NOAH BUILT HIS ARK IN THE SUNSHINE

JAMES W. MOORE

Noah Built His Ark in the Sunshine

DIMENSIONS
FOR LIVING

NASHVILLE

NOAH BUILT HIS ARK IN THE SUNSHINE

This book is printed on acid-free, elemental-chlorine-free paper.

Library of Congress Cataloging-in-Publication Data

Moore, James W. (James Wendell), 1938-
Noah built his ark in the sunshine / James W. Moore.
p. cm.
ISBN 0-687-07538-6 (alk. paper)
1. Noah's ark. 2. Christian life. I. Title.

BS658 .M66 2003
248.4—dc21

2003008514

Scripture quotations, unless otherwise noted, are from the New Revised Standard Version of the Bible, copyright © 1989, by the Division of Christian Education of the National Council of the Churches of Christ in the United States of America. Used by permission.

Scripture quotations marked NKJV are taken from the New King James Version. Copyright © 1982 by Thomas Nelson, Inc. Used by permission. All rights reserved.

Scripture quotations noted KJV are from the King James or Authorized Version of the Bible.

Scripture quotations noted NEB are from *The New English Bible.* © The Delegates of the Oxford University Press and The Syndics of the Cambridge University Press 1961, 1970. Reprinted by permission.

Scripture quotations marked RSV are taken from the *Revised Standard Version of the Bible,* copyright 1946, 1952, 1971 by the Division of Christian Education of the National Council of the Churches of Christ in the United States of America. Used by permission. All rights reserved.

03 04 05 06 07 08 09 10 11 12—10 9 8 7 6 5 4 3 2 1

MANUFACTURED IN THE UNITED STATES OF AMERICA

For

Gary and Dale

Bob and Cynthia

Tommy and Susie

CONTENTS

INTRODUCTION
Noah Built His Ark in the Sunshine

Noah built his ark in the sunshine; in other words, he prepared in advance for the storm that was to come. He didn't wait until the last minute. He used the days in the sunshine to get himself ready. He used those bright days to build up the resources he would need when the dark floodwaters came. The great people of faith have always done that. A good example is Dietrich Bonhoeffer, the noted German theologian who is one of the most quoted people in our time. He was executed in a Nazi prison camp on April 9, 1945. He had been captured and imprisoned by the Gestapo because of his commitment to God, his resistance to Hitler, and his opposition to the Nazi movement.

In prison and concentration camps for two years, Bonhoeffer was a great inspiration to the other prisoners because of his unwavering courage, his confidence in the Lord, his unselfishness, his goodness, and his deep spirit of thanksgiving and gratitude to God, even in that kind of horrible, imprisoned existence.

He inspired even the Nazi guards. In fact, some of the guards became so attached to him that at the risk of their own lives, they smuggled out of prison his papers, poems, and prayers written there, and they even apologized to him for having to lock his cell door after his daily round in the courtyard.

Bonhoeffer's main concern in prison was to be a pastor to his fellow prisoners. He preached to them, taught them, led worship services, counseled them, and ministered to them in their sickness and sorrow. His ability to comfort the anxious and depressed was nothing short of amazing. God was with him, using him and working through him, and somehow people sensed it. For Dietrich Bonhoeffer, every day, even a day in prison, was a day for serving God, thanking God, and sharing God with others.

Before his execution Bonhoeffer, as a prisoner of war in a concentration camp, wrote a poignant and powerful morning prayer in which he thanked God for the restful night, for the new day, and for God's faithful blessings. He asked God to give him strength to handle that difficult situation and still be faithful in his discipleship. He prayed that God would enable him to be strong in his faith, his hope, and his love. He remembered to God his loved ones and then closed his morning prayer with this incredible statement:

> "Lord, whatever this day may bring,
> Thy name be praised!"

Think of that last statement . . . "Lord, whatever this day may bring, Thy name be praised!" The apostle Paul said the same thing in his first letter to the Thessalonians. He wrote, "In everything give thanks; for this is the will of God in Christ Jesus for you" (1 Thessalonians 5:18 NKJV). In both Bonhoeffer and Paul, we see strong examples of spiritual commitment and maturity.

But the question is, how do *we* get there? How do we reach that level of spiritual maturity? Obviously, we all can't be Bonhoeffers or Pauls. How do we get to the place where we can praise God in whatever comes and thank God in everything?

That kind of faith and spiritual maturity doesn't just happen overnight. We have to grow it! We have to work at the faith, practice it, express it, study it, share it; and as we do, our faith will grow, and our gratitude will deepen.

After hearing Bishop Gerald Kennedy preach, a young man said to a friend, "If I could have faith like Gerald Kennedy's, I would be a Christian." To which his friend replied, "Yes, but that faith didn't just happen overnight; he has been growing it for over forty years."

Did you know that psychologists tell us that thanksgiving is learned? You have to learn to be grateful. You have to *grow* spiritual maturity.

The story of Noah is helpful here. Of course, you know that the Noah story has been used in all sorts of ways down through the years. For example, I have a friend in Little Rock who says that his state is the only one mentioned in the Bible, and it is in this story: "Noah looked out the *ark and saw...*"!

Another fellow identified with Noah when he wrote these words:

> When Noah sailed the ocean blue,
> He had his troubles same as you;
> For forty days he drove the ark
> Before he found a place to park!

The story of Noah and his ark (Genesis 6:9–9:17) can best be understood when we see it in the total context of the book of Genesis as a dramatic story told to show us how prone people are to turn away from God, and how God graciously gives us another chance, a new start. In the Noah story we see three important things about faith and gratitude and spiritual strength.

First, Noah Built His Ark in the Sunshine

In other words, Noah prepared in the sunshine for the flood that was to come. The people laughed at him; they made fun of him. They told him that what he was doing was ridiculous and unnecessary. The sun was shining; why waste time building an ark? But Noah kept on building, and when the "troubled waters" came, he was prepared, he was ready, he was equipped and able to ride out the storm.

We need to build an ark on our sunny days. We need to prepare now for troubled waters. Somewhere down the road, there is a "flood" waiting for us, and if we haven't prepared, if we haven't built up inner resources, it will sweep us under!

A man once said to a friend, "I need help. I'm losing my sight. I'm going blind, and all the money in the world can't help me. I don't know what to do. I just don't have the inner resources to cope with this. All this time, all these years, I have given my attention and energy to the wrong priorities. I have leaned my weight on things that can't help me now." This man had not built an ark in the sunshine, and when the flood came, sadly he had nothing to hold him up.

Recently I went to visit a woman who had just lost her husband in a sudden and tragic way. I was touched by her faith and spirit of thanksgiving. She said, "Over the years I've heard so many sermons on suffering and been in on so many Sunday school discussions on sorrow, and those experiences at the church are helping me so much now. I know God didn't do this to me. I'm not blaming God. In fact, I know God is with me now as never before. I can feel his presence and strength. I'm so grateful to the church for preparing me for this hour, and to God for being with me in it." She had built her ark in the sunshine, and then when the flood of tragedy and sorrow came, she was ready.

One day an eleven-year-old girl was called by a local radio station and asked to name the amount of money in the radio jackpot. She couldn't name the amount, and she didn't win the money. In despair, she protested that she always listened, and that this was the first day she had not. "Well, why weren't you tuned in today?" the announcer asked. With the logic of her eleven years, she answered, "Because I didn't know you were going to call today!"

The truth is, we don't know when the storm will come. We don't know what the day will bring. But if we have built an ark in the sunshine, we can say—and mean it—"Lord, whatever this day may bring, your name be praised." Noah built an ark in the sunshine, and so should we.

Second, Noah Let God Close the Door

Noah went into the ark and let God close the door behind him, and he trusted God to open it again. Noah didn't know what the future held, but he knew God was his future, his hope, and his salvation. And in childlike surrender, he let God close the door and trusted God to reopen it in God's own good time and way. This kind of obedient, childlike trust is a basic element in real spiritual maturity.

There are times in life when we don't have all the answers—when we, like Noah, don't know the future, and we have to fall back on God and trust him. This is what Jesus taught, isn't it? "Trust in God! Leave the unseen future in God's hands. He will open the door when the time is right."

Dietrich Bonhoeffer exhibited this kind of trusting spirit. It was the source of his strength. One of his friends once said of him, "He was a giant before men because he was a child before God."

Noted poet Ralph Waldo Emerson, reflecting on the death of his son, Waldo, wrote these significant words, "All I have seen teaches me to trust the Creator for all I have not seen." Noah let God close the door and trusted God to reopen it.

Third, Noah Fell on His Knees in the Mud and Thanked God

Isn't it interesting to note that when Noah came out of the ark, the first thing he did was build an altar to God (Genesis 8:13-20); that is, he thanked God for his deliverance and for God's presence with him. Real, mature thanksgiving is not dependent upon the number of possessions we have. Those are "frosting on the cake." Genuine Christian gratitude praises God for his greatest gift—the gift of himself!

A sanctimonious preacher stood up to preach on Thanksgiving Day and said, "Let us give thanks for good health." Twenty people who were sick left the church. He continued, "Let us give thanks for our homes," and ten people who had no homes left the church. "Let us give thanks for beauty and wonderful minds," he said. Ten more people left who felt they were neither beautiful nor brilliant. "Let us give thanks for friends," he said. Ten people left who felt they had no friends. "Let us give thanks for justice," he intoned. Five people left who felt no justice.

Finally, the preacher looked out, and there was nobody there. The congregation had gone, and the sanctuary was empty. Then he heard the still, small voice of God saying, "When have I promised wholeness of body or health or earthly comfort? When have I promised friends or beauty or intelligence? Remember my servant Job! Remember my son Jesus!" And the preacher cried out, "Then, O Lord, what will you give us?" And the voice of God replied quietly, "Myself." The preacher then ran to the doorway and cried out, "O my friends, I have deceived you. We may have health and friends and justice, but all we are sure of is God!" All we are certain of is God.

Of old, it was said by Job, "Though he slay me, yet will I trust in him" (Job 13:15 KJV). And much later, in his dying, our Savior Jesus spoke to his Father, "Into thy hands I commend my spirit" (Luke 23:46 KJV).

For this is all that is sure—that God gives to us himself, and this is all that matters, this is all that counts. So the preacher said, "Let us give thanks that God himself is with us, world without end." And the people cried, "Amen!" And there was joy in heaven.

Noah built his ark in the sunshine. Noah let God close the door, and he trusted God to reopen it sometime down the way. And Noah fell on his knees in the mud and thanked God, praying, in effect, "Lord, whatever this day may bring, you are here, you are in it, you are with us; so your name be praised."

1

Building the Ark of Spiritual Strength

There Are Some Things You Can't Borrow

Scripture: Matthew 25:1-13

Some years ago, a man came to my office. He was deeply troubled. It was obvious. You could see the pain in his face. He said, "I need to talk. O God, help me, I need to talk! I feel so empty, so dried up inside. I'm scared and lonely and frustrated." He paused for a brief moment, looked at the floor, and then he continued, "I have just come from my doctor's office. I drove straight here. I didn't know where else to go. The doctor told me that I have a terminal illness. I have six months, maybe a year, to live."

Then he added, "As the news sank in, I realized sadly that I have no spiritual resources, no spiritual strength to face this. I have nothing to fall back on, nothing to lean on." He said, "Some people think I'm wealthy, and materially, I am, but that doesn't matter now, does it? Really and truly," he said, "I'm poor in the things that count most. I see it now. All my life, I have put my faith in all the wrong things. The real truth is, I'm spiritually destitute."

He paused again, and then, as if he were thinking out loud, he pointed to the phone on my desk and said, "You know, I could pick up that phone and call any bank in this city and borrow any amount of money to do whatever I want. Just on my name, I could borrow…" His voice trailed off. He leaned forward and put his head in his hands. Tears were streaming down his face. Then, very quietly, he whispered, "I guess there are some things you just can't borrow—and I don't have any of those things."

"Let's go to work on that now," I said to him. "Let's use the time you have left to work on your faith and your friendship with God."

We did that. We built an ark of spiritual strength for him, and thirteen months later he died, but he died with courage and dignity and confidence in God. At the beginning of that thirteen-month faith pilgrimage, I shared with him the scripture for this chapter, the parable of the ten bridesmaids in Matthew 25. He had a sharp mind, and he quickly realized that the parable was about preparing ahead of time for the troubles of life—building up spiritual resources in advance that will give you the strength you need when the crisis unexpectedly explodes into your personal world.

The setting of the parable is a wedding celebration. In biblical times, a wedding party was one of the greatest of all festivities in a village. Everybody turned out. Men got off work, women put aside their household chores, children were excused from their lessons, and all went to the wedding and remained for the celebration.

Now, the high point of the wedding day came when the groom took his new bride from her parents' house to their new home. Here's how it worked. After the ceremony, the bride and groom would enter the home of the bride's parents, perhaps to discuss the dowry. When all the business matters were settled, then the bride and groom would run out joyfully and head to their new home, and the celebration would begin. They would take the longest route possible through the village to make the wedding parade last as long as possible. Here's where the parable picks up.

The young bridesmaids are waiting for the groom to come out

and bring his bride home. But there is an unexpected, long delay, and the girls fall asleep. But then at midnight, there is a shout. The girls wake up. It's the announcement that the big moment is near. "Get ready! Get ready! Won't be long now! The bride and groom will be coming out very shortly!"

However, in the story, some of the young women, who have been waiting all day for this crucial moment in the wedding celebration, now have a big problem. They had not anticipated the delay. They had not counted on a problem. They had not prepared in advance well enough. And now they have run short of oil for their lamps. Frantically, they try to borrow some oil, but they can't, so they rush off to get more oil in a different location, only to find on their return that they missed it! The big moment has passed. The celebration parade is over, the doors to the banquet hall have been shut, and they missed out because they were not adequately prepared!

The point is clear: When crisis comes, you'd better have prepared in advance, because there are some things you just can't borrow! When the crucial moments come, you have to take responsibility for your own life. You have to have your own resources. It's good to have borrowing power. It's good to have material wealth. It's good to have friends to lean on. But sometimes it boils down to you; you have to stand on your own two feet!

The businessman who came to my office that day had learned it the hard way. Jesus had taught it long ago: When crisis comes, there are some things you just can't borrow at the last minute. Here are three examples.

First of All, When Crisis Comes, You Cannot Borrow Somebody Else's Commitment to the Bible

Of course, you could borrow someone's copy of the Bible, but when trouble comes, you need your own Bible, your own biblical strength and knowledge, your own personal biblical inspiration. You need the Scriptures inside of you, written indelibly on your heart. You need your own Bible that you can read daily, marking passages that have special meaning for you, writing your own thoughts in the margin.

Just a few days ago, I went to a funeral. A dear friend of many years had died. In the memorial service, the minister conducting the service held up the Bible that had belonged to my friend. It was held together with silver duct tape! My friend had read that Bible so much, opened those pages so many times, studied those passages so fervently, that she had to use strong duct tape to hold her Bible together. Verse after verse, she had highlighted with a pink magic marker. And in the margins of her Bible next to the great promises of God recorded there—the great promises of God to always be with us come what may—my friend had written, "This I count on." And when this great crisis came that eventually ended her days on this earth, she was ready and faced it all with grace and confidence and courage, and with the strength that comes from spending a lifetime learning and loving the amazing truths of our Scripture.

Let me ask you something: How is it with you right now? Are you at home in the Scriptures? Are you on good terms with your Bible? Is it a trusted friend? Or is it a stranger? Well, let me tell you something. When crisis comes, you need a friend! In desperation, people have turned to the Bible for strength, for comfort, for reassurance, for the Word of Life; and sometimes, sadly, they come up empty, because they don't know how to find its treasures.

Edward Blair, in his book *The Bible and You* (Abingdon Press, 1953; page 52), points out that "the person who is looking for a way to master the Bible in three easy lessons will be disappointed.... In the first place, one can never master the Bible; one can only be 'mastered' by it. In the second place, the Bible is so immeasurably rich that the human mind cannot possibly embrace it all in a few attempts.... Familiarity with the Bible comes only by long exposure ... to its contents

coming to it with an open, alert mind;
respecting the individuality of the writers and the inspiration
of God;
trying to understand what the words meant then and what they
mean to us now;
reading in historical context;
and applying those truths to our own lives today."

When you see it like that, you realize that you could no more hastily borrow someone else's commitment to the Bible in a time of crisis than those young bridesmaids in Jesus' parable could hastily (at the last minute) borrow someone else's oil for their lamps.

There's an old story about a minister who is visiting one day in the home of some of his church members. They ask him a question about where something is located in the Scriptures. He asks if he can see their Bible so he can show them. The mother asks the little five-year-old daughter, Jennie, to "go into the den to the coffee table and bring back our favorite book, the one we love so much, the one we love most of all, the one we read all the time." Jennie runs out, and in a moment she comes back with the Sears catalogue!

Think about that: What is the "favorite" book in your home? What is the one you love most of all and read all the time? Be honest now. How long has it been? How long has it been since you spent some time with your Bible? That's number one: When crisis comes, you cannot borrow somebody else's commitment to the Bible.

Second, When Crisis Comes, You Cannot Borrow Somebody Else's Commitment to Prayer

Some months ago, just a couple of weeks before we left on our vacation, I began to have some pain in my lower back, and then the pain started running down the outside of my right leg. Macho-style, as men will do, I "toughed it out" for a while, but the condition became so painful that we had to come back from our vacation to see my doctor. He checked me over and took some X-rays, but they were not totally conclusive, so he sent me to a back specialist. I went to the back specialist knowing and dreading that he was going to say those three little initials I have come to dislike so much. Sure enough, he said them: "MRI."

Have you ever had an MRI, a Magnetic Resonance Imaging? They slide you into a tube and take magnetic pictures. The pictures are incredible, miraculous, wonderful, but the MRI experience is not wonderful for some people. Sixty-five percent of the population has no trouble at all, but about 35 percent of the people of the world have claustrophobia, and for those folks, MRIs are no fun at all. They are the pits! Unfortunately, not only am I in that 35 percent, I am near the top! I can get claustrophobic, *big time!*

Up to that point in my life, I had endured four MRIs. They all came when I was having my knee problems a few years ago, and after the last one, I said, "I will never do that again!" But then my new back doctor, who is a legend in his field, said, "Let's get you set up for an MRI. That will show conclusively what the problem is." I told my doctor about my last MRI experience, and he said, "Will you try it for me? If you can't do it, you will be in good company, but the pictures are so helpful. So would you try it for me? I'll give you some medication to relax you." I told him that I had tried that once before and it didn't help much, but, okay, for him I would try.

The next day, I showed up for my MRI filled with dread. My appointment was for 3:00 P.M. on that Saturday. My wife, June, and I got there at 2:30. I filled out the necessary papers, and they took me in early. I quickly took the oral medication they gave to relax me, knowing it would not have time to work. But when I got into the MRI room and lay down on that little bed that slides you into the tube, I looked at my watch—it was ten minutes till three—and suddenly, I felt this incredible sense of peace. They slid me into the chamber. I closed my eyes, quoted Scripture, said prayers, and I felt so peaceful.

Twenty minutes later, they slid me out, and—I can't believe I'm saying this to you, but—I could have stayed in there another twenty minutes! I came out to the waiting room and told June that I made it just fine, and she said, "You won't believe what happened. Richard came by, and we had a prayer for you." Richard is a layman in our church who makes hospital calls for us on weekends. He had finished his calls at Methodist Hospital and was cutting through the ER waiting room to take a shortcut to another hospital, and he just happened to see June sitting there. He asked what was going on. She told him about my MRI. Quickly, he said, "Let's say a prayer. An MRI can be claustrophobic, and I know how that is." And standing there in the waiting room, Richard and June held hands and prayed for me. I said to June, "What time was that?" And June said, "It was at ten minutes 'til three"—the precise moment I had felt that amazing sense of peace! I know some will say, "Aw, it was the medication," but I believe with all my heart it was the power of prayer!

Now, let me hurry to say that my back is fine now. I do have a herniated disk, but it's minor, and I'm fixing it with exercise— and prayer. My options are surgery, rest, or exercise, so I'm exercising like crazy, and it's working.

You know, we all need that, don't we—the prayers of others, the prayers of those who love us. Having someone else pray for us is a beautiful thing, a powerful thing; but it's not enough. In addition, we need to have our own personal prayer life.

The best definition of prayer I know of is this: "*Prayer* is friendship with God." That means we don't have to change our tone of voice. We don't have to use pious words or sanctimonious phrases. We just talk to God like we are talking to our best friend—sharing with him our joys and sorrows, our victories and defeats, our concerns, our gratitude, and our fears.

That is real prayer—being with God and recognizing how important God is in our lives, spending time with him as a friend. That's prayer, and you can't borrow that.

Third and Finally, When Crisis Comes, You Cannot Borrow Somebody Else's Commitment to Christ

Recently, the Holocaust Museum in Houston had an elegant luncheon to present their "Guardian of the Human Spirit" awards. Awards were presented to the *Houston Chronicle* and to one of our church members, Jack Blanton. June and I get to go to a lot of nice events in Houston and in the state of Texas because of Jack, who is often and appropriately recognized and honored for his great leadership in our city and state.

Because Jack was one of the honorees, I was asked to come and be on the program. Jack always takes care of us and sees to it that we get to sit with his family. There were twelve people standing around our table, and we recognized everybody there except one couple. "Who is that man?" I asked somebody, and the answer came back, "That's Luci's husband." I wanted to say, "Luci *who*?" but thankfully, I didn't.

Later, as we were being seated, someone said, "Just sit anywhere you would like, but Luci's purse is in this chair, so we will let her sit here, and everybody else, just find a place." I wondered, *Who in the world is Luci?* Moments later, I found out. The event hosts recognized a long list of honored guests—someone from the governor's office, the mayor pro tem, senators and legislators, members of the city council, survivors of the Holocaust. And then finally, the master of ceremonies said, "And of course, we are delighted to have with us today Luci Baines Johnson"—daughter of the late U.S. President Lyndon Baines Johnson—and with that, the Luci at our table stood up! And I thought *Oh, that Luci!*

She was delightful! She asked about our church and told me that she had visited it several times for weddings, funerals, and once for Sunday worship, and she said, "It is always such an exciting experience to be in St. Luke's." I loved that!

I asked about her mother, the former First Lady, Lady Bird Johnson. Mrs. Johnson had had a stroke the previous spring, but Luci said that she was doing better. In those first days after the stroke, Mrs. Johnson could not communicate, but she later improved to the point that she could, with effort, communicate with her family. Luci said to me, "I want to tell you an amazing story." She said when her mother had her stroke, she sat beside her bed each day, held her hand, and said, "Mother, I'm going to pray the Lord's Prayer...." She prayed. No response from Mrs. Johnson.

Luci did that again every day for several days. Still no response. On the Saturday before Pentecost Sunday she did it again, and this time Mrs. Johnson tried to join in. She moved her lips but no words came out. On Sunday, Pentecost Sunday (the birthday of the church, the celebration of God's gift of the Holy Spirit), when Luci held her mother's hand and began to pray the Lord's Prayer, Luci said, "Our Father..." and clear as a bell, Mrs. Johnson said, "Who art in heaven." Later that day, Luci told the doctor what had happened and asked, how was her mother able to do that? And the doctor replied, "Because she has been saying those words for eighty-four years!"

Mrs. Johnson has had her own personal commitment to Christ for all these years, her own ark of spiritual strength. And now, when crisis has come, she has the grace and strength that comes from years of practicing her faith. The poet put it like this:

Thou shalt know Him when He comes
Not by any din of drums,
Nor the vantage of His airs,
Nor by anything He wears.
Neither by His crown,
Nor His gown,
But His presence known shall be
By the holy harmony
Which His coming makes in thee.

Do you know that holy harmony? You can't borrow it. It only comes from a personal encounter with the Living Lord, a personal friendship with Christ our Savior.

Let me conclude with this. A man once came to a farmer and asked to be taken on as a hired hand. "What can you do?" the farmer asked him. The man replied, "I can sleep when the wind blows." The farmer thought that was a strange answer, but he needed a worker, so he hired him. Soon after, the farmer went away on a trip. A couple of weeks later, the farmer returned home one night and went to bed. But a storm came up. Winds were blowing and lashing. The farmer woke and heard the winds, and he remembered the broken barn door, the weak place in the fence, and some ripped wire in the chicken coop. Concerned about his livestock, he got up and went out into the storm to check on them, and what do you think he found? The barn door, the fence, and the chicken coop had all been repaired. The animals were all safe, and the hired worker was sleeping soundly. Then the farmer remembered what the man had said, "I can sleep when the wind blows." This was true because he had prepared ahead for the storm. He could sleep through the storm.

The question is, *Can you?*

2
Building the Ark of Compassion

We Can't Be Too Caring, but We Can Be Too Careful

Scripture: Mark 5:25-34

D r. Fred Craddock is without question one of the great preachers and teachers of preaching in America today. He is the Bandy Distinguished Professor of Preaching and New Testament, Emeritus, at the Candler School of Theology at Emory University in Atlanta. Dr. Craddock is in his mid-seventies now, but he is still active, and is still teaching and preaching.

He tells about an experience he had not long ago in a big supermarket. His wife was out of town, so he decided to fix what he calls "one of my big meals." He went to the supermarket to get a jar of peanut butter. He was in a hurry. The store was huge, and he could not find the peanut butter, so he began to look around for someone who could help him find the peanut butter aisle. He spotted a woman who was pushing her cart along in a confident stroll, and Dr. Craddock thought, *She looks comfortable here. I'm sure she can help me. I'll ask her.*

He walked over to her and asked, "Do you have any idea where the peanut butter is located?" The woman with the cart jerked around, stared at Dr. Craddock, and said, "Are you trying to hit on me?" Dr. Craddock said, "No, I'm not trying to hit on you. I'm trying to find the peanut butter." The woman walked away in a huff.

Then Dr. Craddock saw a stock boy, and he asked him, "Where's the peanut butter?" "Aisle five, way down on the left," came the reply. Dr. Craddock went down to aisle five, and sure enough, halfway down on the left were jars of peanut butter. He reached out and pulled one off the shelf. Just at that moment, the woman with the cart strolled by, and she said, "Well—you *were* looking for the peanut butter." Dr. Craddock replied, "I *told* you I was looking for the peanut butter." And she said, "Well, nowadays, you can't be too careful." Dr. Craddock responded, "Lady, yes you can. Yes you can" (*Craddock Stories* [Chalice: St. Louis, 2001], 45-46).

Now, strange as it may sound, when I first heard Dr. Craddock's peanut butter story, it made me think of this woman in Mark 5 who had had this flow of blood for over twelve years. Under the premise of "We can't be too careful," look at what her society was doing to her. Under the concept of "We can't be too careful," this innocent woman was being shunned and ostracized and abused by society.

She was a battered person, terribly in need of compassion. As far as we know, she had not been battered physically, but without question, she was being battered socially, emotionally, and spiritually by the world in which she lived. They told her she was dirty, and that everything and every person she touched she contaminated and made unclean. It was written into their law. Remember these tough words from Leviticus 15: "When a woman has a discharge of blood that is her regular discharge from her body, she shall be in her impurity for seven days, and whoever touches her shall be unclean.... Everything upon which she lies... everything also upon which she sits shall be unclean.... Whoever touches anything upon which she sits... shall be unclean, and shall wash his clothes, and bathe in water, and be unclean until the evening" (verses 19-27).

Think about that. Her society told her harshly that she was

filthy, and that they couldn't be too careful with her. But even worse, they told her that God was angry with her and that he had sent this misfortune on her, because in their minds they believed she had done some terrible thing to displease him. Of course, they were wrong about that, but they laid guilt and shame on her by the buckets-ful. She was labeled unclean and treated with contempt. Why? Simply because she was sick, simply because she had this unmentionable problem, simply because she had had this flow of blood for twelve years.

For twelve long years her society had battered her. They wouldn't let her go to parties or to weddings or to the market-place or to church. They wouldn't let her go anywhere where she might touch another person. They were saying, "You have this embarrassing problem, and we can't be too careful with you." But think of what that kind of treatment would do to you emotionally, mentally, socially, and spiritually. This woman was tremendously in need of a little compassion and a little caring. And then one day, along came Jesus. Let's look at the story in Mark 5 (also told in Luke 8) together.

Jesus was on his way to see a little girl who was critically ill, when suddenly he was interrupted. As he was moving through the streets, people began to press in around him. The New English Bible puts it dramatically: "He could hardly breathe for the crowds" (Luke 8:42). The people were so excited to be near Jesus that they were pushing and shoving and crowding in close to him. This woman who had been hemorrhaging for twelve years wasn't even supposed to be out there in the crowd, but she was desperate, so she was there.

She slipped up behind Jesus, working her way through the crowd, and when no one was looking, she reached out tenta-tively, fearfully, and touched the hem of his robe. Right then, the story tells us, her bleeding stopped. She thought she had pulled it off. She thought she had gone unnoticed, so she dropped back and tried to lose herself in the huge crowd.

But then, suddenly, Jesus stopped. He turned around and said,

"Who touched me?" (see Luke 8:45). The disciples were astonished by the question. "Who touched you? What do you mean who touched you? *Everybody's* touching you. In this crowd, everybody's touching everybody! What kind of question is that?" But Jesus knew that it was a special touch.

He began to look around. The woman had not expected to be found out, but timidly she stepped forward and told Jesus everything—about this bleeding that had gone on for so long, about how she had tried everything, but nothing had helped, and in fact, she had only gotten worse. She told Jesus that she had heard about him and his power to heal, and how she felt that if she could just touch his clothing, she could be made well. And it had worked. It had worked! The bleeding had stopped.

Jesus' heart went out to her, and he spoke to her tenderly: "Daughter, your faith has made you well; go in peace, and be healed of your disease" (Mark 5:34).

Now, in this fascinating story, we see the compassionate spirit of Jesus, and we discover a crucial lesson for life—that we *can't* be too *caring,* but we *can* be too *careful.* Let me bring this closer to home by looking with you at how this story in Mark 5 underscores the incredible healing power of caring and the importance of building an ark of compassion in our own personal lives. Three ideas emerge gracefully out of this story.

First of All, Caring Has the Power to Bring Healing Physically

Scientific research is now confirming what many of us have suspected all along—that love and compassion and caring do play a big part in the healing process. Let's be honest and quick to say that sometimes the healing happens in this life, and sometimes it happens in the life to come. But whenever and wherever it happens, it is without question the result of love and compassion and caring.

Dr. Patrick Doyle was a physician in Canada. He had to give

up his medical practice because of a debilitating illness. He retired and moved to a small lumber town in eastern Canada. He did not open up a new practice, but word got around that a doctor now lived in the community. He would go and visit people in their homes, and people were grateful for any service or medical advice he could provide.

When Dr. Doyle first came to town, he met a fifteen-year-old boy by the name of Johnny Lake. Johnny knew everybody in town and could, and did, talk to everyone. Johnny became Dr. Doyle's unofficial nurse and helper. One night Dr. Doyle received a telephone call. It was from the Owens family. They lived only two blocks away. Their daughter had been sick for a number of days and now seemed to be getting worse.

Dr. Doyle went to their home and examined little Kathy. It was clear that her situation was very grave. He guessed that she had pneumonia. He didn't have the medicines or the means with which to treat her condition, and other professional help was just too far away to reach in time. He told the parents their daughter probably would not make it through the night.

Dr. Doyle was exhausted. He had had a long, difficult day, and he said, "I'm going to go home and rest a bit, but Johnny will stay here with you." And Johnny did. Oh my, did he!

It was after midnight when Dr. Doyle awoke, and he went back to the Owens's home. When he walked in he noticed Johnny was right beside little Kathy's bedside. He was holding her hand and talking to her constantly. He was saying, "Breathe, Kathy, breathe. When springtime comes, we'll make dandelion chains. Breathe, Kathy, breathe. When springtime comes, we'll make buttercup wreaths. O God, please help Kathy breathe. When springtime comes, Kathy, you and I will go and stand on the bridge over the creek and we'll try to count the minnows in the creek. Breathe, Kathy, breathe."

Dr. Doyle whispered to the parents, "How long has this been going on?" They said, "He's been talking constantly to her for two hours. She got to the point where she was gasping for breath, and there were long periods when there was no sound at all. Several times we thought she had died. But Johnny has been talking to her through the whole thing. Her breathing seems to be much more regular now. Doctor, isn't there something you can do to help?" Dr. Doyle said, "Me? No. I'm not about to interfere with a miracle. Your daughter is going to be okay."

This true story reminds us first of all that caring has the power to bring healing physically.

Second, Caring Has the Power to Bring Healing Socially

Did you wonder why Jesus called attention to the woman? Why didn't he just let her slip away and get lost in the crowd? Because by bringing her forward and announcing to the huge crowd that she was healed, he was saying to the people: "Look now! She is well! She has been healed! God is not angry with her, so stop shunning her. Let her reclaim her place in the community. Widen the circle, and let her in."

You see, he had healed her physically. Now, he was healing her socially. He was restoring her to an active role in normal society of that day. He was reconciling her with her community.

One of the most amazing books I have ever read in my life is Ernest Gordon's book *Through the Valley of the Kwai*. Ernest Gordon writes about his experience as a prisoner of war in Thailand during World War II. He tells about how the Christmas of 1942 was so radically different from the Christmas of 1943. In 1942, the prisoners were selfish and self-centered. They robbed the sick and mistreated one another. They didn't care whether the other prisoners lived or died. But during the following year, a healthy American soldier began giving his food to a sick buddy to help him get well. In time, the sick prisoner recovered, but the buddy who had given him food died of malnutrition.

The story of the man who gave his life for his friend made the rounds of the camp. Some of the prisoners began to talk about how Christlike that was. They remembered verses of Scripture they had learned years ago under very different circumstances. After that, some of them began to live in the caring spirit of Christ, and the whole prison camp was transformed. They built a church in the jungle. They had Bible studies. They prayed together. They built a hospital where they could care for the sick, and make medicines from the plants, and make crutches from the trees for those who needed them. They started caring for one another and helping one another. The entire spirit of the camp changed from despair to hope, from selfishness to compassion. And when Christmas of 1943 came, two thousand prisoners gathered for worship. They sang carols and read the story of Christ's birth; but more, they shared their food, and they shared the love of Christ with one another—all because one man came into that prison camp and lived his faith. They were reconciled, made new, socially healed, made one family, all because one man lived in a way that reminded them of the caring spirit of Jesus Christ.

Caring has the power to heal us physically and socially.

Third and Finally, Caring Has the Power to Bring Healing Spiritually

At Barbara Bush's literacy conference here in Houston in the spring of 2002, one of the featured authors was Dr. Ronan Tynan. You may recognize that name. He is one of the world-famous Irish tenors. In addition to commenting on his book, Dr. Tynan was coaxed back onstage to sing "Danny Boy," and then with everyone standing, he sang "God Bless America." It was magnificent.

In his book *Halfway Home: My Life 'til Now,* Ronan Tynan shares his remarkable story of overcoming adversity and attaining worldwide success in several different areas. He is an award-winning singer, an award-winning athlete, an award-winning horseman, an award-winning doctor, and an award-winning writer.

His accomplishments are even more amazing when you realize that he was born with a serious lower-limb disability, causing him to spend the first three years of his life in the hospital and to have his legs amputated when he was twenty years old.

How did Ronan Tynan do it? How was he able to accomplish so much while standing, walking, and running on prosthetic legs? He credits his friends, his teachers, his family, and his faith, but especially his father, who encouraged him and supported him and affirmed him and loved him day-in and day-out. Ronan Tynan said that the teasing and narrow-minded comments of some people did get to him, but they didn't stay with him, because he always remembered his father. That's what kept him going—the love and affirmation and encouragement of his father.

Well, let me tell you something. We have a heavenly Father who loves us like that and then some—a heavenly Father who encourages us, affirms us, supports us, loves us, and cares for us more than we can imagine. And his caring is so powerful that it can bring healing—physically, socially, and spiritually.

Our calling as Christians is to imitate God's loving Spirit daily. And if we are to do that well, we need to build an ark of compassion now.

3
Building the Ark of Peace
Strong Faith for Tough Times

Scripture: Mark 5:1-20; John 16:25-33

I t is always sad when nations go to war. In recent years the sadness has been magnified, because just a little more than a decade ago, we seemed so close to a lasting peace. The wall had gone down in Berlin. Eastern Europe had opened up. The Cold War with Russia had thawed. And at that time, in the early 1990s, we thought, *Finally! At long last, we can have a peaceful world.* But then suddenly on August 2, 1990, Iraq invaded Kuwait, launching a crescendo of tension-packed events that led to the Persian Gulf War. Then, more than ten years later, we experienced the horror, tragedy, and heart-wrenching pain of September 11, 2001, which led to the War on Terror, prompting military action in Afghanistan and now again, as I write these words, in Iraq. And over the course of these last few dramatic days, unforgettable images have captured our minds and touched our hearts.

For example:

- the image of people by the thousands coming to kneel at the altar of our churches to pray for peace, joining hundreds of thousands of people around the globe in peace prayer vigils;
- the image of a grandmother leaving our sanctuary last Sunday and asking us to pray especially for her grandson, a jet pilot stationed somewhere in Kuwait, because, she said, "If war breaks out, he will be one of the first to see action";

- the image of a little preschool-age girl saying on television, "I hope we don't have war, because people might get hurt";
- the image of world leaders and congressional leaders and people in the streets agreeing that something should be done, but strongly disagreeing over how to do it;
- the image of television newscasters suddenly realizing while on the air that the war had started;
- the image of people all over the world stopping what they were doing and gluing themselves to their television sets for hours and hours;
- the image of President Bush speaking to the nation and to the world from the Oval Office;
- the image of one young soldier showing four different crosses he was wearing constantly around his neck, sent to him by different friends and relatives, and then saying, "In foxholes, there are no atheists," and another young Marine wearing around his neck a piece of debris from the World Trade Center;
- the image of courageous TV and radio news correspondents giving the news in dangerous situations and then scurrying to safety or frantically helping each other put on gas masks;
- the image of two little girls crying because their mother was in the military and was stationed in harm's way in the Middle East;
- the image of seeing war, as never before, on live television.

On and on we could go with a moving and poignant litany of these powerful images etched indelibly into our hearts and minds. Now, I don't want to be overly dramatic or sensationalistic, but I do think this is what we are concerned about in these days. I do think this is the elephant in the room that doesn't seem to ever fully go away. I do think we need to grapple with this together. I do think we need to try to bring some spiritual light to the situation.

Let me admit up front that I am certainly no authority on this complex matter, and I do not pretend to be. Back during the 1960s, a woman reporter asked Elvis Presley what was his solution regarding the war in Vietnam. Elvis answered, "Ma'am, I just sing songs!" In like manner, I just preach sermons, and I know less about war than Elvis did. But I feel that something needs to be said on the subject, so let me give it a try.

Over the years as I have studied the Bible, Christian theology, and history, I have noticed that broadly speaking, there are four basic approaches to war. Let me briefly and simply outline them, and you see if you can find yourself and your view somewhere between the lines.

First, there is the *Holy War* approach. Holy War advocates believe strongly that their war is of God, that their military crusade is divinely ordained and divinely inspired. The Holy War crusaders are absolutely certain that their convictions are right because they firmly believe that they are fighting for God. Many wars in history have started with this kind of religious fervor.

One of the most tragic examples of the Holy War mind-set occurred in the Middle Ages when a group of 20,000 children (some of them no more than twelve years of age) becames convinced that God wanted them to wage a military crusade. They marched off to war, never to return. Many were killed, and others were sold into slavery.

And then, there is always that haunting question, What if both sides believe they are doing God's will? Once when war broke out, one of our military leaders was asked, "Is war of God, or is it of Satan?" Soberly he answered, "It's of man."

A second approach to war is called *Pacifism*. Of course, the basic premise of the pacifist position is that there is no such thing as a Holy War. "All war is unholy and immoral," says the pacifist. The view here is that violence of any kind is utterly unchristian. The pacifist maintains that if you really search the mind of Christ and think deeply about the meaning of Christian love, the conclusion you come to is that violence, force, and killing are incompatible with discipleship.

However, the arguments that the pacifists have to wrestle with are obvious:

What do you do when someone invades your home and threatens to do harm to you and your family?

Or what do you do when someone abuses an innocent and defenseless country?

How do you deal with the aggressor?

How do you resist what is evil or hostile or wrong?

This brings us to a third approach, which some have labeled the *Just War*. The basic premise here is that war is always a tragedy and should always be a last resort. Every effort at negotiation should be tried. Yet, when these fail, there are occasions, say the Just War advocates, when war becomes necessary.

Thomas Aquinas, in the thirteenth century, said that a just war must satisfy three conditions: It must be declared by public authorities, the cause must indeed be just, and the motive must be right.

During World War II, William Temple expressed the just war philosophy when he said this: "We [Christians in wartime] are called to the hardest of all tasks: to fight without hatred, to resist without bitterness, and in the end—to triumph without vindictiveness."

A new element that recently has been brought into the Just War approach is what is called "Humane Fighting." *Humane Fighting:* Sounds like a contradiction, doesn't it? But what it means is that force should be directed only toward the destruction of armaments. Innocent lives should be protected as much as possible: "Take out their weapons!" Instead of wholesale attacks on a nation without regard for the civilian population, use surgical, precision strikes to destroy their military weapons. Render them weaponless—and then they will come to talk peace.

Of course, the problem here is that it's impossible to employ that much force and only take out hardware. Casualties will occur on both sides, and when the casualty happens, it will be somebody's son or daughter, somebody's wife or husband, somebody's father or mother.

Now, a fourth approach to war has emerged in recent years

because of the advent of modern weapons and the frightening threat of nuclear power. It's called *Waging War by Sanctions*. We have heard a lot about this in recent years. The idea here is that military force is too dangerous and too destructive, and a better way to deal with the problem is to cut the troublesome nation off from international supplies. Cut them off from the world and weaken them in that way, to the point that they *have* to come to the peace table. We have heard the pros and cons of this approach in Congress and elsewhere in recent years.

Now, what do *you* think? Where do you stand? Are you a crusader, a pacifist, a just war advocate, or someone who believes we can wage war with international sanctions?

By the way, I have different Christian friends who strongly subscribe to each one of these different positions—and they all base their view on their Christian faith, and they all document their approach with Scripture. So, it can be very confusing. And yet in the complexity and perplexity of it all, I do see some important lessons begging to be learned. I hope and pray that the present war is very short, and that our soldiers are safely home very soon. But as we go through war and try to move beyond it, I hope we will think about these things.

First of All, More Than Ever, We Should Realize That Our World Has Become a Global Village

Because of the amazing advances in travel and telecommunications, we have become a global village. We live in a rapidly shrinking world. With every passing day, especially because of television satellites, we become more and more aware of one another, and our lives become more and more interrelated with those of people around the world.

The lesson is obvious. We in the world must stop seeing other nations as enemies, and rather see them as neighbors with whom we share our global village. If you have any doubts about that, let me document it.

I was watching an ABC newscast. A news correspondent was interviewing one of the highest-ranking officials in Saudi Arabia. The conversation was sober, serious, businesslike, until the Saudi official suddenly heard a familiar sound on his earphone. Suddenly the Saudi official became very animated, very excited, and then the following conversation took place.

"Wait a minute! Wait a minute!" said the Saudi official. "Was that Ted Koppel's voice I just heard?"

"Yes."

"May I say hello to Ted?"

"Of course."

"Ted Koppel, is that really you? I watch you every night. You are great! Keep up the good work. I can't wait to get home tonight to tell my family I talked to Ted Koppel!"

That Saudi official was like a kid in a candy store, so thrilled to hear the voice of Ted Koppel, a television celebrity he watches every night.

Also, have you noticed that when some new development occurs in war, leaders of nations all over the world are watching CNN to see what really happened? Often, CNN is giving news to the world even faster than national intelligence agencies can get the scoop.

A couple of years ago when our travel group toured China, we visited a Chinese kindergarten. The children performed songs for us in their native language. Then their teacher, who could speak a little English, asked us to perform for them. Since the kindergarten was connected to a farm, we sang, "Old MacDonald Had a Farm." When we finished that first line, guess what those Chinese kindergartners did. They shouted back to us, "E-I-E-I-O!"

We live in a global village, no question about it. And we need to see other nations and other peoples as neighbors, and not enemies. In this war, even though we may not understand the Iraqi leaders and the things they do, we must not permit ourselves to hate the Iraqi people, because they too are God's children, and they too are our neighbors in God's global village called Earth.

A Second Important Lesson Is This: People in Our World May Seem So Very Different, but Fundamentally We Are So Similar

Our languages may be different; our clothes may be different; our customs may be different; our physical traits may be different; our worship may be different. But the truth is, basically we are pretty much the same. The common people, the people on the street, the "regular folks" like you and me in every nation are very similar.

I have not traveled as extensively as some people I know, but I have been to England, Belgium, Germany, Russia, France, Israel, Jordan, Greece, Japan, Egypt, China, Italy, Turkey, Canada, Mexico, Spain, Portugal, Singapore, the Scandinavian countries, not even to mention Waxahachie, Texas; and everywhere I have been, I have discovered that people, in every nation, are so much alike. They love their children. They are concerned about healthcare, education, and food for their tables. They worship, they pray, and they do not want war.

Recently in our church's sanctuary, we hosted a worship service for unity. People were here from many different cultures, nationalities, and backgrounds. Greeks, Romans, African Americans, Hispanics—even some native Texans were here. It was a touching, moving experience, and I found myself thinking not about how different we are, but rather how alike we are. God must have loved variety; he made so much of it! And yet deep within us, there is an incredible kindred spirit, an amazing alikeness, which comes from being brothers and sisters in God's family.

There has been a lot of talk about economics in this war. The debate rages, "Is it over aggression or is it over oil?" But let me invite you to think about the economics of it all in another way. Dream with me for a moment. If we in this world could somehow learn how to get along, just think what we could do. If we didn't have to spend so much time, effort, energy, creativity, and money on defending ourselves from one another, just think what we could do. If all the nations of this world could learn to live together in peace without the threat of war, we could take those incredible resources and wage war on hunger, homelessness, disease, illiteracy, and drug abuse. I know it sounds idealistic. I know it sounds like the impossible dream, but I can't help thinking about it. Just think what could be done. Just *think* what could be done.

Third and Finally, the Most Important Lesson of All Is, Jesus Christ Is the Prince of Peace

I believe with all my heart that the way to a lasting peace resides in Jesus Christ—in what he came for, and stood for, and died for; in his intense pursuit of truth, love, and justice. That is precisely what this story in Mark 5 is all about. Christ walks into the tormented life of the Gerasene demoniac, this madman who is at war with everybody, and whose life is coming apart at the seams, and Jesus turns it around for him. He gives this man the healing he needs and brings peace to his troubled soul.

At the beginning of this narrative, it sounds like a horror story. This is an eerie, grim, suspenseful situation. Jesus and his disciples have just come through a storm on the Sea of Galilee. It is nighttime, and having survived that frightening storm, they are thrilled now to set foot on solid ground. But as they get out of the boat, they encounter a different kind of storm. Yet another scary experience. They hear strange sounds coming from the tombs—shrieks, growls, screams, moans, the rattling of chains. Then suddenly, there appears a horrifying sight: an adrenaline-filled madman in tattered clothes, bruised, dirty, bloody, and battered, with pieces of chains dangling from his arms and ankles, screaming and running directly toward them!

Now, let me ask you something: What would you have done in that situation? This was a perilous place; a blood-curdling moment; a powerful, dangerous, berserk man was charging them. I think I would have run for my life, or jumped back in the boat. But not Jesus! Jesus stood his ground and faced the madman, undaunted and unafraid. Jesus stood there and dealt with this wild man. Jesus healed him. Jesus brought peace to his troubled soul. He changed him, cleansed him. Jesus turned his life around. And you know, don't you, that he can do that for you and me, and he can do that for our world.

Please notice something here. The madman said his name was *Legion*. That's a military word, and so appropriate in this case, because this man was at war. He was at war with himself. He was at war with other people. He was at war with God, and Jesus, the Prince of Peace, healed him. Jesus, the Prince of Peace, gave him peace within, peace with others, and peace with God.

He can do that for you and me. And he can do that for our world, which today is so like Legion, so desperately in need of peace within, peace with others, and peace with God. Remember how Jesus put it in John 16:33 "In the world you have tribulation; but be courageous, for I have overcome the world" (author's paraphrase). This means that Christ endured the worst this world can dish out and was victorious over it. This means that what he represented cannot be defeated. His truth cannot be killed; it resurrects! His love cannot be stopped; it endures! God cannot be defeated; ultimately God wins, and through faith in him, the Peace, the Healing, the Victory, the New Life can be ours.

4
Building the Ark of Christian Love

Being More Than Conquerors

Scripture: Romans 8:37-39

Don and Frances Scherer are two of the most devoted members of our church. They were so proud of their grandson, Donald. Donald, twenty-four years old, had taken a job as youth director at a church in Corpus Christi. With the vitality of his own youthfulness and his deep commitment to Christ, he was doing a magnificent job in reaching the young people there, and he was leading them in a healthy direction. His faith was contagious, and the young people were catching it. Donald was so excited and so enthusiastic about what was happening.

One weekend, he drove home to Houston to share his joy with his parents. He drove all the way to Houston to tell his parents how much he loved his new job and his new church and his new opportunity to "make a difference" in the lives of young people. He told them how much he loved those young people. He told them he had found his place, his calling, his purpose in life. He told his parents that he knew he would never become wealthy as a youth director, but he didn't care about that because he had found his treasure, "a better treasure," in getting to work with those youth.

Donald left Houston that Saturday night to head back to

Corpus Christi. He was to help lead the worship services the next morning and to be with the young people in Sunday school. But he never made it. At 2:00 A.M. on Interstate 59 near El Campo, Texas, everything changed. Donald had no warning, no way of knowing as he drove under the overpass at Highway 71, that a twenty-two-year-old young man, who had had too much to drink at a just-closed dance hall, had only moments before pulled onto the highway going the wrong way.

They hit head-on, both going sixty to seventy miles per hour. There were no tire marks, which meant there had been no time to apply the brakes, no time to react or even face the pain. But even in the awful rubble of that tragic accident, the paramedics found signs and symbols of Donald's laughter and sense of humor, his love for God, his love of life, and his love of young people. In the car they found a silly-looking jester's hat (the symbol of his youthful fun and playfulness). And they also found at that tragic scene two of Donald's Bibles, with passages underscored and highlighted, and with pages worn from constant reading and study, prompting the paramedics to say, "He witnessed to us from the wreckage."

One of the paramedics was so touched that she took the time to sit down and write a letter to Donald's family. This beautiful and poignant letter is so moving that I want to share it with you word-for-word, in its entirety.

Dear Scherer Family,

My name is Phyllis Hodges. I am a paramedic with El Campo EMS. I was on duty the morning of your son / brother's death.

I felt compelled to write you about the circumstances that have touched me. I was in the first ambulance that responded to the collision. When I arrived, it was obvious that there was nothing we could do for Donald. However, we know that his death was instant and he did not suffer.

Although I cannot tell about his last moments, I can assure you that he was surrounded by Christian men and women at the scene treating him with the utmost respect and dignity. While walking around Donald's vehicle, I noticed two Bibles on the side of the road. How did they get there? I do not know. I looked at the books to see if there was any information that might be useful for the police and EMS report. I was amazed to see the amount of underlining in the first Bible. My thought was: here is a young man that knew Jesus. The other book was very well read, with plenty of wear and tear to the text.

The responders also noticed the jester hat and beads in Donald's vehicle. It was not until I went to his website that I found out that Donald was also known as the joker. We knew that this young man, not knowing his age or anything about him, *loved life and loved the Lord!* Even though we did not know his destination, we knew he had *gone home to God!* Please know that even in Donald's death, he was witnessing for Christ.

Donald's death has made me wonder that if I died today, would the responders know that I, too, was a Christian? My plan is to do something about that. I hope that I can use his life as an example. I want to make sure that I always have Christ with me, not just on Sundays. I am so very sorry for your loss. I know that your grief is unbearable at this time. I hope realizing that others are praying for you will bring you some measure of comfort. *Jeremiah 31:13* [which contains these words: "I will turn their mourning into joy, / I will comfort them, and give them gladness for sorrow."]

Donald's loss is a heart-wrenching tragedy to his family, to his church, to his young people, to his friends, and to all of us who knew him. But at the same time, his loss reminds us of the apostle Paul's powerful words in Romans 8. Paul wrote: "In all these things we are more than conquerors through him who loved us" (verse 37). Some would say Donald was defeated by that accident on Interstate 59, but we know better, don't we? We know he wasn't! We know strongly that his great Christian spirit made him more than a conqueror: It made him not a victim, but a victor!

A few verses later in Romans 8, the apostle Paul put it like this in one of the greatest statements in all of the Bible. Paul said that we are more than conquerors because nothing, not even death, can separate us from "the love of God in Christ Jesus our Lord" (verse 39). Donald was "more than a conqueror," and that's what we are called to be.

Her name was Joleen. She was stricken with cancer when she was sixteen years old. During the next three years, she and her family made over forty trips to the hospital. There was a lot of pain, a lot of discomfort, a lot of broken dreams, a lot of disappointments. But through it all, Joleen never lost her faith. She never lost her smile, never lost her sense of humor. Finally, she died, just nineteen years old! Just before she passed away, I went again to see her. She said something to me that I will never forget. Realizing that her time on this earth was short, she said, "Jim, for three years now you and others have prayed and prayed that I might be made well, that I won't have to suffer anymore." She smiled, took my hand, and said, "Soon now, your prayers will be answered. I'm going to be made well. The suffering will be over, and I'll be with God! I'll miss my family and my friends, but I'll be with God, and I will be well!"

Some would say cancer defeated her, but it didn't! It didn't, because her indomitable Christian spirit made her not just a victim, but a victor. At her funeral, when I read this passage from Romans 8, I accidentally put the emphasis on the word *more*, and the text took on a fresh meaning, especially as I reflected on Joleen's life. We are *more* than conquerors! We can't always win in this world, but we can, with the help of God, always be more than conquerors. The message of our Christian faith is that with the spirit of Christ, we can be victors, even when we are victims.

Have you heard about the young man who wanted a job as an usher in a movie house? The owner was interviewing the young man to see if he could handle the usher job, and he asked him, "Son, what would you do if the theater caught on fire?" The young man answered, "Well, sir, you don't have to worry about me; I'd be the first one out of here!"

That was not the answer the owner was hoping for, because, you see, that's not enough! The young man would have conquered the situation and saved his own skin, but as an usher, *more* is expected of him than that.

Remember the temptation experience of Jesus in the wilderness (see Matthew 4:1-11; Mark 1:12, 13; Luke 4:1-13). Jesus had gone there early on to meditate and pray, and to think through the kind of ministry he should have. There in the wilderness, Jesus was tempted in three different ways to become a conqueror. He was tempted to become a powerful economic liberator, a conquering military leader, and a magical wonder-worker. But he resisted all of those temptations and chose instead the way of love, the way of the cross, the way of the suffering servant. Jesus refused to overpower or overwhelm or coerce people with brute force. You see, Jesus chose to be more than a conqueror.

Remember the rich young ruler (see Matthew 19:16-30; Mark 10:17-31; Luke 18:18-29). He was a conqueror. He had won out in the financial world, in the world of success, leadership, and power. He had clout! He was a rich, young ruler—a conqueror. But look! It is not enough. There was something lacking in his life. Wealth, youth, and power were not enough! Winning was not enough. There was a vacuum, a hunger, an emptiness. Jesus saw it and said to him, "Follow me and I'll give you something more fulfilling. Follow me and I will make you more than a conqueror!"

Listen! Christ is trying to tell us something. Christ is showing us, as a baby in a manger and as a Savior on a cross, that the happy people, the fulfilled people, the genuine people are not the bullies, not the power mongers, not the selfish people, not the mean-spirited people. Christ is calling us to be more than conquerors, to be merciful and humble and thoughtful, to be considerate and patient and kind, forgiving and loving. Of course there are times when we have to defend ourselves and others, but basically Christ is teaching us to walk through life gently and graciously so that we don't selfishly elbow other people out of our way, or push or shove or grab or possess.

Now, let me hurry to say that this doesn't mean weakness; it means *strength*—the strength of bigness and love, the magnanimity and courage to choose to be more than conquerors! Let me be more specific and bring this a little closer to our daily lives.

First, As Christians, We Are Called to Be More Than Conquerors in the Home with Our Children

Some parents approach parenthood as "conquerors." They see their children as things to be conquered or as problems to be controlled, rather than as persons to be loved.

Sometimes in the counseling room, we hear children and young people exclaim, "If just once my parents would say 'thank you' or 'please' to me, I would feel more like a human being. If only they would treat me like a person with feelings."

Some years ago when our son Jeff was born, I can remember standing in the corridor of the hospital one night, looking in the nursery window with my nose pressed against the glass, admiring our new little boy. A woman came over and asked, "Is that your baby?" I proudly answered, "Yes!" And then she said, "Isn't that something; he looks just like a little *person*!" I thought to myself, *He is! That's exactly what he is—a little* person! But sometimes we parents forget that, don't we? We forget that children are persons, and we give way to the temptation to treat them as things to be conquered.

Recently I was having lunch with a friend of mine who happens to be a child psychologist. At the next table there was a young woman who was having a terrible time with her daughter, a young preschooler who looked to be about three years old. They had obviously been shopping, and the little girl was tired and sleepy. She spilled her water, and she dropped her spoon, and she got some food on her dress. The mother was scolding her and jerking her impatiently and slapping at her and talking to her in a very hostile tone, calling her "stupid."

As we left the restaurant, that mother and daughter were standing by the door, and my friend stopped. He felt so sorry for the little girl, that he knelt down in front of her and said to her, "You know, you are a very special little girl, and I like you!" He patted her on the shoulder, and she smiled. As he stood up, the mother wasn't smiling! She cut her eyes toward him and said, "You don't approve, do you?" My friend looked at the woman and said, "Well, it's just that I'm a psychologist, and I know what you are doing to this child!"

Now, let me ask you something. What are we doing to our children? How do we treat them? How do we relate to them? How do we view them—as things to be conquered, or as persons to be loved? Please don't misunderstand me. I am all for good, loving discipline. It's one of the best ways to express love and to give children security. But I'm talking here about attitudes— and I simply want to remind us that as Christians, we are called to be more than conquerors with our children.

Of course, this can be turned around. Some children and youth are guilty here, too. They forget that *parents* are people too. Some children and youth view their parents as things to be conquered or outwitted or tricked, and that's just as bad. Christian love means being "more than conquerors" in the home.

Second, As Christians, We Are Called to Be More Than Conquerors with Our Mates

It has always bothered me, whether on the college campus or in the high-school corridor or in the business office, to hear men talk about their sexual conquests. The word *conquest* is a revealing word, isn't it? The very word sounds sacrilegious because it arrogantly refers to another human being as a kind of object, an accessory, a plaything to be conquered, used, and discarded. There is something very unchristian about that!

Just as wrong is the woman who, figuratively speaking, holds her man on a string and displays him, like a fisherman showing off prize catches—catching and conquering, and breaking hearts along the way. It's wrong, because we are called to be more than conquerors.

And too, there are many married couples who spend their entire married life in competition with each other, vying for power and position, trying to get the upper hand, each partner trying to conquer the other.

Once, a couple came to see me. They had been married less than a month, and already they were having a harsh disagreement. I took the man aside and said, "Look, Tom, it's not worth it. For the sake of your marriage, why not give in?" He said, "Oh, no! I can't do that! I can't let her get the upper hand in this, or I'll be henpecked!" Then I took *her* aside and asked her if she could give in, for the sake of the marriage, and she answered, "Oh, no! If I let him have his way in this, he will take control and boss me around for the rest of our days!" Their marriage lasted about six months, because they didn't understand how to be more than conquerors with their mate.

Third and Finally, As Christians, We Are Called to Be More Than Conquerors with God

Some people try to conquer God. They want to put God in their pocket like a rabbit's foot. Some of us want God to be like a genie in a bottle, where we can control him and keep him safely tucked away until we need him, and then we let him out to do us a special favor. Some try to master God and make him their ever-ready servant, rather than their sovereign Lord.

But, you see, this misses the point. We can't conquer God. History documents this over and over. God won't be defeated! When he was a baby, they tried to kill him. When he became a man, they tried to kill him. But God's truth can't be killed. It resurrects! It lives on! It endures! Even when he was a victim, he became a victor.

One of the most beloved legends of Christmas is that of the little drummer boy. When the Christ Child was born, many beautiful gifts were brought to the manger, so the story goes— gifts of great beauty and splendor. But one small boy was very poor. He had nothing to offer the Lord, and this made him very sad. Then he thought, *I can play my drum for him!* And so he did. *Pa-rum-pum-pum-pum. Pa-rum-pum-pum-pum.* He played with all the love in his heart, and as he played, according to the legend, the Christ Child smiled, showing that the gift of love is the best gift of all!

So if you want to bring a smile to the face of Christ, don't go through life beating up on people, but rather beat the drum of love. Go out into all the world in his Spirit—and be more than a conqueror!

5

Building the Ark of Strong Foundations

Fixed Points in a Changing World

Scripture: Matthew 7:24-27; Hebrews 12:25-28; 13:8

The noted author Lloyd C. Douglas once described a fascinating visit he had one day with an old friend. His friend was an elderly man who had been a highly respected music teacher for many years. Lloyd Douglas greeted the veteran music teacher with this question: "Well, Professor, what's the good news today?" Now, that's a fitting question for us to think about these days in our turbulent world. How would you answer that? What do you think is the good news today?

Well, the elderly musician made an interesting response to that question. Without hesitation, he went over to a tuning fork that was suspended from the ceiling by a silk chord, and he struck it with a soft mallet, producing a pure and beautiful tone. Then, with an expression on his face that reflected awe, wonder, and reverence, the old professor listened with deep appreciation to that single music note as it floated gently across the room, and finally he said, "That, my friend, is 'A.' It was 'A' all day yesterday. It will be 'A' all day tomorrow. It will be 'A' next week and for a thousand years. Indeed, it will be 'A' forever. The soprano upstairs warbles off-key, the tenor next door flats his high notes, and the piano across the hall is out of tune. But that," he said, striking the tuning fork again, "is 'A.' And that, my friend, is the good news for today."

Now, what did he mean by that? Simply this. The good news for today is:

There are some things in this life that we can always count on.

There are some things in this life that are pure and eternal. They do not change.

There are some fixed points in this ever-changing world.

Navigators can always count on their North Star. Builders can trust their plumb lines. Scientists can rely on their square roots. And musicians can depend on their set notes. There are some things in this life that are constant and solid and unshakable.

That is precisely what this passage in Matthew 7 is all about. It is located at the end of the Sermon on the Mount, and Jesus is telling us here to build our lives on a strong foundation, to build our lives on the things we can always count on. And that is also precisely what the strange-sounding passage in Hebrews 12:26-28 is all about. It reads, in part: " 'Yet once more I will shake not only the earth but also the heaven.' This phrase, 'Yet once more,' indicates the removal of what is shaken—that is, created things—so that what cannot be shaken may remain. Therefore, since we are receiving a kingdom that cannot be shaken, let us give thanks."

Then, notice this. Just a few sentences later, we find the same thing said in an even more powerful way in one of the "mountain-peak" verses in the Bible. Hebrews 13:8 says, "Jesus Christ is the same yesterday and today and forever." Jesus Christ is the same; that's good to know in this turbulent, stormy, tumultuous, swiftly changing world in which we live, a world in which there is no totally safe haven, no place completely insulated from the changes. To paraphrase Robert Frost, the way out is the way through.

Psychologists tell us that change is often quite hard on us. It's threatening, frightening, and intimidating, and there is just one way that we can adjust to change successfully. They teach us that when the changes come, we should remember some fixed points in life, to which and by which we can orient ourselves; some fixed points we can trust and believe in and commit to; some fixed points we can always count on because they do not change.

Little children learn early this need for fixed points. That's why when they face a change or go into a strange new situation, they quickly grab their security blanket or their teddy bear or their thumb or their mom or dad. Frightened, they want something tried and true that they can hold on to, an ark they know they can count on and trust.

On a deeper level, the question is, what are the fixed points for us as our world shudders and shakes, as we go through trying times. Well, Jesus Christ, the same yesterday and today and forever, helps us immensely here. Some have said that Jesus came and turned our world upside down—and we know what they mean. But really, I think it's the other way around: He came and turned the world right side up! Jesus came and showed us in his life and death and resurrection the things that really matter, the things that are eternal, the things that are pure and everlasting and unshakable, the things that will stand the test of time, the things that are of God, the things that will take us through this challenging time and will still be here, strong as ever, when the turbulent times are over.

Jesus Christ came to give us some fixed points in a changing world, an ark of strong foundations. There are many of them. Let me underscore three, and I'm sure you will think of others.

First, There Is Truth

Truth is a fixed point—a strong foundation—and when we know the truth, it does indeed set us free. However, the problem is that it is sometimes very difficult to sort out what is true. This is particularly the case in these modern times. How do we tell what is truth and what is propaganda, or what is a blatant lie?

For example, the Pentagon describes an event one way, and then someone in the Middle East goes on television and says just the opposite. Obviously, someone is playing loose with the truth, but eventually the real truth will come out. The message is clear: We have to be very careful in our pursuit of truth.

Have you heard about the man who one day asked his wife, "What was the best time, your favorite time, in your life?" She answered thoughtfully, "I think it was when I was uh, uh six." A few days later the woman's birthday arrived, and her husband told her that he had great plans for her on her special day.

He woke her up bright and early, and off they went to a local amusement park. He took her on every ride—the roller coaster, the Death Slide, the Screaming Loop, the Wall of Fear—they did it all. Five hours later, she staggered out of the theme park, her head reeling and her stomach churning. Then her husband took her to McDonald's. He ordered her a Big Mac, extra fries, and a large chocolate milk shake. Then he took her to a movie, the latest Hollywood blockbuster, and he bought her a hot dog, some popcorn, a coke, and some M&M's. What a day! Finally, she wobbled home with her husband, and, exhausted, she collapsed across the bed and wearily closed her eyes. Her husband, so proud of himself, sat down beside her and lovingly asked, "Well, dear, what was it like being six again?" One eye opened, and she said, "I meant my *dress size!*" The moral of the story is if a woman speaks and a man is actually listening, he will *still* get it wrong!

Now, that's a light treatment of a very serious subject. How do we "get it right"? How do we keep from getting it all mixed up? Especially these days! With all the conflicting ideas bombarding us today and vying for our allegiance, how do we know the truth?

Well, we need a fixed point for truth. We need a measuring stick, and that is one of the things Jesus Christ does for us very well. He is our measuring stick for truth. In the beginning of John's Gospel, Jesus is referred to as "the Word." The Greek word is *logos,* and in John it means the will of God, the mind of God, the idea of God, the purpose of God, the intention of God, or, put another way, the truth of God. And his truth is marching on.

If we want to know how wide my desk is, there is only one way to know for sure: We measure it with a dependable measuring stick. That's what Jesus Christ does for us. He is the measuring stick for truth. We need to measure everything we see or read or hear by the standard of truth we see in Jesus Christ.

If we hear someone speak words that are mean-spirited, shout words that are hateful, scream words that are cruel, mutter words that are prejudiced, spew out words that are profane, then we can be sure that they don't measure up to the test of Jesus Christ. He is the measuring stick for truth, and his truth is a fixed point we can always count on.

Second, There Is Love

Love is another fixed point we can always trust. Jesus taught that emphatically, in word and deed. In the way he lived and in the way he died, he epitomized the power of love. If we in this world could somehow capture the spirit of Christ, if we could all learn to live together in love and good will, just think what we could do, just think what we could accomplish.

When the famous writer F. Scott Fitzgerald died, he left among his papers the plot of a play that he never wrote. It was a simple story about five people who lived in various parts of the world. They all inherited one house. However, there was a condition: They all had to live together in the house!

Without question, this is the plot for our shrinking world today. And without question, the hope for our world today is found in Jesus Christ and the love he embodied. He shows us what God is like and what God wants us to be like, and the word for it is *love.*

We are all familiar with the name Babe Ruth. He was one of

the greatest baseball players of all time. "The Babe," as he was affectionately called, hit 714 home runs during his baseball career. Unfortunately, he played too long. He continued to play when he had gotten older, and his ability had waned, both at bat and in the field.

There's a story about how during one of his last games as a professional, the aging Babe Ruth had a terrible day. He made several errors. In just one inning, his errors were responsible for five runs scored by the opposing team. As Babe Ruth walked off the field after that disastrous inning and headed for the dugout, a crescendo of boos and catcalls was directed at him by the angry crowd. Babe Ruth had never known a moment like that. The fans who had loved him for so many years had turned on him with a vengeance. It was a painful and humiliating moment for this great athlete who had been the number one star of baseball for so long.

But just then, a little boy in the bleachers couldn't stand it. He couldn't bear seeing Babe Ruth hurt like that. The little boy jumped over the railing onto the playing field, and with tears streaming down his face, he ran toward Babe Ruth. He knelt before his hero and threw his arms around the player's legs. Babe Ruth picked the little boy up and hugged him tightly.

Suddenly, the noise from the stands came to an abrupt stop. There was no more booing. In fact, an incredible hush fell over the entire ballpark. The boy's love for Babe Ruth had melted the hearts of that hostile crowd. Love happened in right field, and suddenly the outcome of a baseball game didn't seem that important anymore.

Truth and love are fixed points in this changing world—fixed points we can always trust and always count on. They bring us back to reality.

Third and Finally, There Is God

God, of course, is the most important fixed point of all. He is the one constant that we can always depend on.

A June 2002 decision of the 9th U.S. Circuit Court of Appeals called the Pledge of Allegiance unconstitutional because it refers to "one nation *under God*" [emphasis added]. This reminded us, once again, that the debate over the separation of church and state is ongoing. But it is clear what our nation's founders believed about that. They believed that they were the instruments of God in shaping and forming a new nation, a nation under God, a nation based on trust in God.

A *Newsweek* survey of June 29, 2002, revealed that 87 percent of Americans—almost nine out of every ten—did not want the Pledge of Allegiance changed, and 87 percent of Americans believed it was acceptable for government to promote religious expression, as long as no specific religion is mentioned. Only 12 percent of those polled thought the government should eliminate all reference to God and religious belief in government settings. And the majority of Americans thought that it was good for the country when government leaders publicly express their faith in God.

We need a little common sense here. A few years ago in New England, a rabbi was asked to pray at a middle-school graduation. The rabbi tried his best to pray a prayer that would not be threatening to anyone or to any group. He simply gave thanks to God for the legacy of America, where diversity is celebrated and the rights of minorities are protected. A lawsuit followed, and the prayer was ruled unconstitutional. The court suggested (are you ready for this?) that the prayer would have been fine if the rabbi had left out all references to God!

Now, please don't misunderstand me. I know that we have great diversity in our nation. I know that we are multicultural and multiethnic. I know that we now have more than twelve hundred different religious bodies in our country. I know that there is a need for respect and understanding with regard to our religious differences. But I also know about our faith heritage as a nation, and that a nation's identity is shaped by morality, and that morality comes from faith.

How can we debate big ethical issues like nuclear arms or the death penalty or cloning or drug problems without reference to religion? How can children be truly educated without any reference to our spiritual heritage? It's impossible! So much of who we are goes back to the great lessons of the Bible. So many of our present-day laws go back to the Ten Commandments. So much of the civilizing process is rooted in the doctrines of faith. And so much of the best of what we are (in my opinion) goes back to the life and teachings of Jesus. The very idea of removing all references to religion from American life absolutely distorts our understanding of the influence of faith on American culture, and it prevents people from drawing on our country's rich and diverse religious heritage for guidance.

So the point is clear. If we build on the strong, unshakable foundations of truth, love, and God, then we can weather any storm!

6

Building the Ark of Churchmanship

Why Go to Church?

Scripture: Isaiah 6:1-8

J esse Ventura has been in the news a lot in recent years. Jesse Ventura used to be a professional wrestler. He then became the governor of Minnesota. In one interview, he had this to say about religion: "Organized religion is a sham and a crutch for weak-minded people who need strength in numbers. It tells people to go out and stick their noses in other people's business."

Ventura went on to say that he considers himself a Christian, and that he believes Jesus Christ is the Savior. But, he also said, "I don't believe necessarily that I need a church to go to. My religious beliefs can be by a lake, they can be on a hill, they can be in the solitude of my own office. And I believe," he said, "that there's no set example of what people's beliefs should be."

Well, what do you think about that? How do you feel about that? When I read about Governor Ventura's remarks (now, let me hurry to say for those of you who are wondering, that I read the interview on the CNN Web page, and not in that notorious magazine where it was first published), I had two immediate responses.

My first response was a bit flippant. I thought to myself, *I'm sure the governor of Minnesota, in his lifetime, has said some bright things, but that was not one of them.*

My second response was more thoughtful. I found myself wishing that I could bring Governor Ventura to Houston and let him experience our church here. I wish he could feel the excitement and the joy and the love of St. Luke's. I wish he could feel what we feel when we walk into church, when we come together into the sanctuary as a church family.

I wish he could walk these halls with me on Sunday morning and see what I see—little children rushing to Sunday school with such joy and exhilaration on their faces, cars and buses and vans circling the parking lot trying to find a place to park, the ushers and greeters welcoming people to church with genuine warmth and affection and kindness, choir members scrambling to get into their robes and scurrying to the preservice rehearsal, young people making their way to church early on a Sunday morning to serve the church even though they were out late on Saturday night, staff members working feverishly behind the scenes to make the worship service warm and welcoming and celebratory, church members greeting and hugging one another and reaching out to visitors with love and respect in the spirit of Christ. I wish I could take the governor to our day school, to our youth fellowship and our "Seniors' Place," to our Sunday school classes and our Disciple Bible study. I wish he could see the glow on the faces of our team members after they have just returned from one of our mission work trips. I wish he could hear our music and see people kneeling at the altar for prayer.

There are so many incredible things, amazing, life-changing things that I would like to show him in my church because, you see, I am convinced that the governor of Minnesota has never seen or experienced a church like St. Luke's. If he had, then I believe with all my heart that his views about the church would be totally different.

You know, of course, that it happens not just to governors, but sadly, it happens to all kinds of people. They have had a bad experience with some narrowly focused, rigid religious group (or no first-hand experience at all with any church), and they throw the baby out with the bath water. But Governor Ventura's comments do raise a significant question that I would like for us to look at in this chapter, namely this: "Why go to church?"

In a Gallup poll that was taken a few years ago, pollsters asked people a simple question: "Did you go to church in the last seven days?" Amazingly, the answer didn't match up with the statistics. More people said they went to church than actually would be borne out by the statistics of average attendance in the churches of America. Gallup could not figure out what had happened. Finally, the conclusion was drawn that many people actually *felt* as though they had been in church, even though they hadn't been there.

The noted religion professor and writer Martin E. Marty worked out a tongue-in-cheek paraphrase of a possible answer given to one of the pollsters who knocked at the door of the home. In this scenario, the homeowner answered the question by saying something like this: "Well, I wasn't actually there in church, but I intended to be there. So put me down as a 'yes.'"

But you see, when it comes to church attendance, good intentions are not enough. Whenever and wherever we joined the church, we stood at the altar and promised God we would support the church faithfully. We promised God that attending church regularly would be a top priority in our lives and in our schedules. Some of the early church leaders called it a "holy habit," and they were on to something, because going to church is a habit, and not going to church is a habit. That's why those early Christians encouraged us to cultivate the holy habit of making church attendance a top priority. That's why churches reaffirm that vow every Sunday with every new member who joins.

But let me ask you something. How are *you* doing? How are you doing in your church attendance? How faithful are you, really, in supporting the church with your presence? Have you built the ark of strong churchmanship in your life and through your holy habits? Let me put that in perspective by asking you some questions.

If your car would start one out of four times, would you consider it faithful?

If your television worked 60 percent of the time, would you consider it faithful?

If your newspaper delivery person should skip your house every other day and an occasional Friday, would you call that faithful?

If your water heater should greet you with cold water three mornings a week, would it be faithful?

If you should fail to come to work five or six days each month—would your employer consider you faithful?

If you should miss a couple of house payments in a year, would your mortgage holder say, "Oh well, ten out of twelve months, that's not too bad"?

If you attend church once or twice a month—25 to 50 percent of the time—would you say that you're faithful?

It's something to think about, isn't it? Now, with all of this as a backdrop for our thinking, let me give you my list of three reasons we go to church, three reasons for going to church that explode out of the Scripture for this chapter in Isaiah 6. In this powerful story, we see Isaiah experiencing the presence of God in the Temple in a life-changing way, and out of that experience, he senses three dramatic things: a closeness to God, a compassion for people, and a call to ministry.

And that is precisely what worship does for us. It draws us closer to God. It gives us a compassion for other people. It calls us to ministry. Let's take a look at these together, one at a time.

First of All, Going to Church Draws Us Closer to God

In his vision, Isaiah came to the Temple that day, and he had one of those mountaintop experiences with God, an experience much too powerful to express in words, an experience that drew him closer than ever to God. Put that over against this. Do you remember how in the New Testament, right after the miracle of Easter, the Risen Lord appeared to the disciples in the Upper Room, and they were absolutely bowled over by this incredible experience of seeing with their own eyes the resurrected Christ? He had defeated sin and death—the most amazing miracle of all time. It was the greatest news of all time, and together, as a church family, the disciples all experienced it. All, that is, except Thomas!

Thomas missed it for one reason and one reason only: He wasn't there! He was absent! Now, we know in his grace and compassion, the risen Lord came back and appeared again later just for Thomas, but it's a haunting story, isn't it? There's a lesson there somewhere, and I think it has to do with this: How many great moments with God have you missed? How many life-changing moments with God have you missed simply because you weren't there, simply because you were absent from church, and simply because you haven't really made up your mind yet to commit your life to God and to church?

Bill Hybels has written a book called *Making Life Work: Putting God's Wisdom into Action*. In it, he talks about commitment to God and to the church, and he says this:

> Soon after I became a Christian, I did what most new believers do: I quietly considered how seriously I intended to take my newfound faith. I realized that Jesus had died for me, and I wanted to show my gratitude by trying to walk with him. But to what extent? I knew I should read my Bible a little bit. I knew I should pray now and then. I knew I should get somewhat involved in my church. But how far did I need to take all this?
>
> I knew a few people who were becoming flat-out, totally devoted... Christians. Almost overnight, it seemed, their faith was altering everything: their morals, their relationships, their money management—and in some cases, even their careers. This seemed a little extreme to me. I was quite sure I didn't want to go that far. But how far did I

want to go? To what extent did I want my new faith to affect my everyday life?

And then Hybels wrote these very important words:

> About that time a mature, Christian man who knew me well sensed my struggle. "Bill," he said, "I have a challenge for you. Why not put your whole life in God's hands? Why not trust him fully? Why not stake your whole life on him? Why not let him lead and guide you in every area of your life for as long as he proves himself trustworthy? If at any point he shows himself to be untrustworthy,...then you can bail, get out, turn your back—whatever. But until that time, give God the opportunity to lead and guide your life. Give him a chance to prove himself trustworthy."

Well, to make a long story short, Bill Hybels did just that, way back, some twenty-five years ago. And you know what he has discovered? He's discovered that instead of shutting his life down and making it boring, just the opposite has happened. It drew him closer to God, and as a result his life is happier and fuller and more exciting today than ever before! Life has opened up for him in some phenomenal ways! And all because, way back there, he decided to commit himself completely to God and to the church.

Let me ask you something. Have you done that? Have you made that decision to trust God and to put God and the church at the top of your priority list? Have you decided to support God and the church with your presence in worship every Sunday? As Isaiah learned many years ago, going to church will draw us closer to God.

Second, Going to Church Gives Us Compassion for Other People

In the Temple that day, Isaiah became concerned about the people. He wanted to reach out and help them. Church, at its best, makes us more compassionate people.

Statistics show that people who go to church regularly are

happier and more satisfied than those who don't. And regular churchgoers live longer, new studies have revealed. Think of that—going to church adds years to your life and life to your years! Regular churchgoers are more loving, more generous, more caring, more gracious, more morals-directed, more honest, more accepting of others. They are less prejudiced, more committed to family life, and more involved in working and serving out in the community to improve the quality of life for everybody, and especially for those who are less fortunate.

Why is that? It's because no institution in the world teaches love and compassion like the church does. Remember that famous remark from Mother Teresa? Someone asked her how she could find the strength to work daily with all those needy people. She answered by saying that she would look into their faces and see the eyes of Christ. She learned that in church. The church teaches us to see every person we meet as Christ in disguise. The church teaches us that we are not isolated Christians. We are family.

One of my favorite poems says it well.

> A thing you cannot do:
> You cannot pray the Lord's prayer
> And even once say "I,"
> You cannot pray the Lord's prayer
> And even once say "my,"
> You cannot pray the Lord's prayer
> and not include another,
> For when you seek your daily bread
> You must include your brother.
> For others are included
> In each and every plea;
> From the beginning of it
> To the end of it
> It doesn't once say
> "Me."

Going to church draws us closer to God and gives us compassion for other people.

Third and Finally, Going to Church Calls Us to Ministry, Calls Us to Serve

That too happened to Isaiah, that day long ago. There in the Temple, he felt the tug of God. He realized that a prophet was needed for that time, and he said, "Here am I, Lord; send me!"

One Friday night I went to a high school football game, and while sitting there in the stands I had a strange thought. I imagined this: You go to a football game. Fifty players huddle up with their three coaches. Suddenly, the referee blows his whistle to start the game, and a crazy thing happens. The fifty players stand there on the sideline, and the three coaches run out onto the field to play the game. Some of the players shout encouragement. "Go get 'em, Coach!" "Put it on 'em, Coach!" "You can do it, Coach!" But none of the players goes out onto the playing field. They expect the coaches to do it all.

If you saw that at a football game, what would you think? You would think, *This is the most bizarre thing I have ever seen!* And yet, that's the way some people relate to the church. They think the ministers and staff are supposed to do it all, while the other church members stand by and watch.

But that is certainly not the biblical example. Think about it. Jesus did not call a single priest or rabbi to be one of his disciples. He called laypeople to help him do his work.

He is calling you right now. He has a special job that only you can do. Can you hear his call? And can you say with Isaiah, "Here am I, Lord; send me"?

Going to church—supporting the church with our presence—that is so important, because it draws us closer to God, it gives us compassion for others, and it calls us to ministry. And it builds the ark of churchmanship.

7

Building the Ark of Christian Witness

"Who Will Be a Witness for My Lord?"

Scripture: Acts 2:43-47

A few years ago, we had the popular singer and concert artist the Reverend Cynthia A. Wilson-Hollins at our church to conduct a lecture series. As always, she was magnificent. Her theme song for the series was a wonderful spiritual that has this recurring line: "Who will be a witness for my Lord?"

Every time I hear that spiritual, I think of the story about the man who was accused of some wrongdoing. He was brought before a judge. The judge asked the man if he had an attorney to represent him. The man answered, "No, I can't afford one." To which the judge replied, "Well, don't you worry about that. I'll appoint a lawyer to represent you, and I will choose a real good one." "I appreciate that, Judge," said the man, "but if you sincerely want to appoint somebody to help me, what I need most is not a real good lawyer. What I really need arc some real good witnesses!"

Well, that's precisely what God wants, too, isn't it? Some real good witnesses! Let me ask you something: Will you step forward and volunteer for that job? That's our calling as Christians—to be God's witnesses. Let's define the term. A good *witness* is one who knows something firsthand, one who has seen or heard or experienced something. A good witness is one who can bring the truth to light.

Well, that is precisely what Simon Peter was doing at Pentecost. He was boldly bearing witness to the truth of God, and he was well prepared to do that because he had built his ark of witness on sunny days. He had been one of the followers of Jesus. He had traveled with him daily. He had heard Jesus preach and teach. With his own eyes, he had watched him perform miracles of healing. He had seen Jesus change peoples' lives dramatically; Peter's own life had been changed. Also, he had witnessed the Crucifixion and the Resurrection. He had talked with the Risen Lord—had even had breakfast with him!—and he had been there when Christ ascended into heaven.

And now, here in Acts 2 on the Day of Pentecost, we read that Simon Peter was empowered by the Holy Spirit, and he stood up to speak out for Christ. So powerful was his witness that on that very day, three thousand people were converted to Christ (see Acts 2:14-42). Peter recommended his Christian faith so convincingly that day that three thousand persons were baptized and brought into the church.

Now obviously, we can't all be as effective as Simon Peter in our Christian witness, but the truth is that through faith and commitment to God, we can all be empowered by the Holy Spirit to recommend our religion to others meaningfully and productively. As we study closely the witness of Simon Peter at Pentecost, three things stand out: the power of well-spoken words; the power of love and inclusiveness; and the power of real commitment to Christ and his church.

To bring this closer to home and make it more intimate for each one of us, let me restate those three ideas in the form of three personal questions. I hope you will grapple with them honestly and earnestly in your heart.

First, Will You Be a Witness for Our Lord by the Way You Speak?

Peter was a powerful, effective, convincing witness that day with words, by the way he spoke. Words are so important.

A word can excite or a word can depress.

A word can make us glad or sad or mad.

Words can inspire and lift our spirits or defeat and deflate our souls.

Words can motivate and encourage or they can crush and kill.

Words can convince us to stand tall for what is right or they can destroy hope and blast reputations.

Words can offer a beautiful prayer and preach a powerful sermon or they can incite a riot or tell a dirty joke.

The words we choose, and the ways we use them, communicate more about us and our faith than we can possibly imagine. Profane words, obscene words, bigoted words, hateful words, cruel words—these do not promote the cause of Christ or represent the spirit of Christ. They never have, and they never will. We dupe ourselves by calling our dirty talk mature, adult, realistic speech. Come on now! What could be more immature, childish, and unrealistic? If you want to be a good witness for Jesus Christ today, clean up your act and clean up your speech. Speak the words of faith, hope, and love in the tone of compassion, kindness, and respect.

Some years ago, when I was a senior in high school and had just decided to go into the ministry, I was sitting one day in the school cafeteria. One of my classmates named Bill sat down beside me and said, "Hey, is it true what I heard, that you are going to be a minister?" When I answered, "Yes," Bill said, "You know, Jim, I've never been to a church service in my life." "Why not?" I asked him. "Well," he said, "I had a bad experience with a church when I was in junior high. My family didn't go to church, and I didn't know anything about it. But I was curious. So one Saturday afternoon when I was in the eighth grade, I went into this church building near my home. I didn't mean any harm; I just wanted to look around. But while I was in there, this man came up behind me. He grabbed me and accused me of trying to steal something. He called me a dirty name, and he ran me out and threatened to call the police. I've never been back to church. I know it's unfair to judge the church by that one experience, but to this day when I think of the church, I think of that man—the look on his face, his attitude, his cruel words—and I shudder."

The point is obvious: We can turn people on to the church or we can turn them out of the church by the way we speak.

Some years ago, when Salvation Army cofounder Catherine Booth died, her body was carried to a great auditorium in London. For hours and hours, people streamed by her casket in an outstanding display of love, affection, and gratitude; by the hundreds they came. One man in that long line expressed what they were all feeling that day. He said, "She spoke to me as no one ever had before. She cared for me, and I could tell it by the way she talked to me. I was an outcast, lonely and lost. I will never forget her voice. There was something so wonderful and so meaningful about the way she spoke to you. You could feel the spirit and love of Christ in her words."

Well, how is it with you? Are people drawn to Christ and to the Christian faith by the way you speak?

Second, Will You Be a Witness for Our Lord by the Way You Treat Others?

One of the most beautiful aspects of the Pentecost story is the way in which it is made clear that Christ is the Lord and Savior for all people of all nations. Medes, Parthians, Egyptians, Romans, Asians, Elamites; and on and on it goes! They are all there. They are all welcome. They are all included. They are all loved and treated with respect. They are all invited to accept Christ and to be baptized in his name. "Whosoever will, may come."

Several years ago, an interesting article, written by Lois Wyse, appeared in *Good Housekeeping* magazine. It listed some bits of advice for women considering marriage, some helpful guidelines for finding a good husband. She said that there are six ways to learn everything you ever need to know about a man before you decide to marry him.

First, she suggested, "Watch him drive in heavy traffic."

Her second suggestion was that you "play tennis with him."

Third, she said, "Listen to him talk to his mother when he doesn't know you're listening."

Fourth, she said, "See how he treats those who serve him (waiters, ushers, maids, service station attendants, and others)."

Fifth, she suggested, "Notice how and for whom he spends his money."

And sixth, "Look at his friends."

And then after sharing those six suggestions, the writer came up with yet another one, almost as an afterthought. "Oh, by the way," she said, "if you still can't make up your mind, then look at his shoes! A man who keeps his shoes in good repair generally tends to the rest of his life, too."

Did you notice a common thread here? Not counting the last one about the shoes, all the rest of these guidelines have to do with how we treat other people. I think the writer is on to something here, something very important. If you're looking for a mate or a friend, look at how that person treats other people. It is so true! The way we treat other people reveals a lot about who we are. It reveals a lot about our faith. The way you treat others tells me the most about your theology. Let me show you what I mean.

I know a man who claims to be very religious. Many people regard him as a man of great faith. He can quote Scripture with the best of them. He can rattle off important dates in church history. He can recite the creeds eloquently. He can spout high-sounding theology into the air. But I'm not impressed, because I've seen how he treats his wife and children. I've seen how he treats his neighbors and those who work for him. He is harsh with people. He is tough and hostile and critical. He's judgmental, ill tempered, and impatient with everyone around him.

All of the outer religious fervor and activity means nothing if we are cruel and hateful toward other people. When we show love, compassion, and kindness to others, that's when they really begin to see our faith. So, if you want to do good for Christ, then treat others with respect and love.

What do you think? Does the way you speak bring others to Christ? And how about the way you treat other people—does that bring them to Christ and the Christian faith?

Third and Finally, Will You Be a Witness for Our Lord by the Way You Serve Christ and His Church?

At Pentecost, people by the thousands became Christians because they saw Simon Peter's commitment to the church. Peter was devoted to the church, and with good reasons. There is no institution in the world that serves people like the church. There is no institution in the world that helps families like the church. There is no institution in the world that redeems lives like the church. There is no institution in the world that teaches love like the church. There is no institution in the world that lifts God up, and inspires righteousness, and cultivates goodness like the church. But even more than that, the church has Jesus Christ!

The world is starving to death for Jesus Christ, and we have him. We are here to share Jesus Christ with a needy world, and everything we do is for that purpose. We have worship services and Sunday school classes, Bible study groups and enrichment groups. We have youth groups, children's groups, singles groups, and mission work groups. We take trips, we put on dramas. We play games, we present concerts. We paint houses, we build clinics. We feed the hungry, and we help the needy, all for one purpose: so we can share the love of Christ, so we can tell people about him. If you want to be a good witness for Christ, if you want to recommend your faith to others, the best thing you can do is to serve Christ and his church with all your heart and soul.

Let me ask you something. Be honest now. What if every church member were just like you? What if every member served the church and supported the church like you do, what kind of church would we have?

Think about this seriously. Does your commitment to Christ and his church inspire others to trust him and serve him and want to give their lives to him? We see this happening dramatically at Pentecost. When Simon Peter stood up to preach that day, he didn't know how it was going to turn out. He didn't know how his words would be received. Would they hear him with hope or hostility? Would they react positively or negatively? Would they fall on their knees beside him or rise up in arms against him? Would they respond in faith and penitence or would they try to stone him to death?

He just didn't know. But he did know that the Holy Spirit was with him. So he did the best he could and trusted God to bring it out right. And God did! And Simon Peter's confident trust enabled others to commit their lives to Christ and the church.

Do you trust God like that? Do you trust God that much? God wants some really good witnesses today. Will you step forward, and stand tall, and be one of them by the way you speak? by the way you treat others? by the way you serve Christ and his church?

8

Building the Ark of
Kairos Moments

The Powerful Moments That Change
Your Life Forever

Scripture: Mark 1:14-18

I am a collector of lists, and I want to share with you my all-time favorite list. It's a list of answers given by English schoolchildren on their religion exams.

One student wrote this, "Noah's wife was called Joan of the Ark."

Another one said, "A myth is a female moth."

Another one said, "The Pope lives in a vacuum."

Another child said, "Sometimes it is difficult to hear in church because the agnostics are so terrible." (There's a sermon there somewhere!)

And I love this one. One student wrote this, "The Fifth Commandment is 'Humor your father and mother.'"

But my favorite one of all is this last one. One student wrote this, and I'm going to use the student's precise words: "Lot's wife was a pillar of salt by day, and a ball of fire by night."

I have no idea what that means!

The point is, right answers are important, aren't they? But have you thought about this: so are right questions! And what I want to do is raise with you what I think is a "right question" for us to be thinking about these days, and the question is this: How

74

long has it been since you had a powerful moment that changed your life forever?

The New Testament originally was written in common Greek, and the Greeks had several different words for our one word *love*. *Agape* is one. That means "unconditional love." It's the word used in the Bible to describe God's love for us. Every time we are talking about the love of God in the Bible, the word *agape* is used—"unconditional love."

Eros is another one. It gives us our word *erotic,* but actually, if you go back and study the original Greek, you'll understand that *eros* really didn't mean "erotic love" so much as it meant "bargaining love"—or "I'll do *this* for you, if you'll do *that* for me" (which, if you think about it, is not really love at all).

Philia is another one. It gives us our word *philanthropy,* and it refers to "brotherly, sisterly love," "humanitarian love."

And another one is *storge,* or "family love."

We all have probably heard that the Greeks had lots of words for our one word *love*. But did you know that the Greek New Testament also had two words for our one word *time*? These are *chronos* and *kairos*. Let me briefly define them for you.

Chronos gives us our word *chronology,* and simply put it means "tick-tock time." Each second is exactly like the one that went before it, exactly like the one that will follow it. *Chronos* time is boring time, humdrum time, drudgery time, meaningless time, empty time. Let me paint the picture of *chronos* time for you like this.

Imagine, if you will, a convicted prisoner in a prison cell, crossing off dates on a calendar; that's *chronos* time. Imagine, if you will, a lawyer who has to argue her case the next morning. It's very important that she be rested and fresh, but she has insomnia, and she cannot get to sleep. All she can hear is the persistent, unrelenting, incessant ticking of a clock. Imagine, if you will, an office worker who hates his job. He can't wait till 5:00 P.M. comes so he can get up and get out of there. Or, imagine, if you will, a college student who is in a three-hour biology lab that happens to occur right after lunch. And that college student is so bored that she can't wait to get out of there and go do whatever college students do out on the campus. *Chronos* is empty time; it's a void that must be filled; it's time we must put in or endure; it's what we talk about when we say, of all things, we were "killing time."

Chronos is "tick-tock time," humdrum time, boring time, and routine time.

Thank God, there is another kind of time. It's called *kairos.* *Kairos* time is "full time," vital time, crucial time, decisive time, God's time. *Kairos* moments are those powerful, extra-special moments in life that are packed with meaning. *Chronos* is ticktock time; *kairos* is when time stands still.

How long has it been since you had a moment so powerful that time stood still? *Kairos* is when God breaks into the routine and speaks loud and clear, and you are touched so powerfully, so deeply in your soul, that you can never be the same again. A cartoonist depicts *kairos* with a light bulb flashing over somebody's head. It is the *Voila!* moment, the "ah-ha!" experience. Theologians call it the moment of revelation.

Kairos is a key word in the New Testament. When Jesus started his ministry, he came into Galilee preaching and saying, "The time is fulfilled, and the kingdom of God is at hand. Repent, and believe in the gospel" (Mark 1:15 NKJV). And the word used for "time" there is not *chronos*; it's *kairos.* This was crucial time, decisive time, redemptive time, God's time.

Jesus' life was packed with *kairos* moments. For example, remember Zacchaeus (see Luke 19:1-10). Jesus saw him in that sycamore tree, which he had climbed to get a better look at Jesus. They connected; it was a *kairos* moment.

Or think of Bartimaeus, who was blind and by the roadside. Nobody else was paying attention to him, but Jesus heard his cries. Jesus connected with him, and it was a *kairos* moment.

And then there was the woman who came up behind Jesus and touched the hem of his robe. (See Mark 5:24*b*-34.) Jesus turned around, and he connected with her, and it was a *kairos* moment.

Jesus had so many of those. The question is, how long has it been since *you* had a *kairos* moment in this *chronos* world? How long has it been since you had a moment so powerful that it changed your life; turned your world upside down; or maybe better, put it right-side up, where you could never be the same again? *Kairos* moments are all around us if we have the eyes to see them, and the ears to hear them, and the hearts to feel them.

Now, let me share with you three *kairos* moments that changed my life forever. And, if you will forgive me, I am going to be very personal, because I have to be; *kairos* moments *are* very personal. So, I want to share with you three very special *kairos* moments that touched me so deeply in my soul that I could never, ever be the same again.

Here's number one.

The *Kairos* Moment of Encouragement

First of all, there was the *kairos* moment of encouragement.

The word *encourage* in French literally means, as noted in a previous chapter, "to put the heart in." How long has it been since you had a *kairos* moment of encouragement where you put the heart in somebody, or where somebody put the heart in you?

It happened on December 17, 1979. It was a Monday morning, a week before Christmas. We were living in Shreveport at the time. I was in the master bedroom. It was 7:00 A.M. I was rushing to get to the office because it was the week before Christmas and we had so much to do, so many things to take care of, so that our people could have a great and meaningful celebration of Christmas. But at 7:00 A.M., the phone rang. June answered it in the kitchen, and I could hear her talking, but I couldn't make out the words. Then I heard her running down the hallway toward the master bedroom, and I knew—I could feel it in the air—I knew something was wrong.

She ran into the master bedroom and said, "Jim, get on the phone quickly, it's your sister Susie, calling from Winston-Salem; your mother was killed in a car wreck this morning."

I couldn't believe it. It was "*déjà vu* all over again" for us, because we had lost our father in a car wreck many years before. I got on the phone with my sister. We were able to conference in my brother from Memphis, and the three of us talked about what had happened.

Mother had gone with her neighbor to take her neighbor's niece to the bus station in downtown Winston-Salem, so that her friend wouldn't have to drive back home alone after they had left the station. The accident happened in a 20-miles-per-hour zone in downtown Winston-Salem. Nobody else was even hurt, but my mother died instantly. We were thrust quickly and painfully into that grief experience. We went through the funeral on Thursday. We had to stay over a few days to take care of business matters, and the next Monday we flew back home and landed at the airport in Shreveport at three o'clock in the afternoon on Christmas Eve. We had a big Christmas Eve service planned at the church that night, a Holy Communion service. In that church we had only one service on Christmas Eve. It was held at 5:30 P.M., and 1,200 to 1,300 people usually would come for that service. I had told the staff that I would be there to help with Holy Communion.

As we were preparing to go to church, I decided to look through the mail. This huge stack of mail was there, with all these wonderful letters and cards of love, sympathy, compassion, and caring. And then, I saw it. I knew what it was. It was a great big box. It had a Winston-Salem postmark on it. I knew before I opened it what it was, and I was right: It was our Christmas presents from my mother, carefully selected and beautifully wrapped, and mailed to us the day before she died. It touched me so deeply that I began to cry, and I said to June, "I don't know if I can do this." She said, "You don't have to. I'll call the church and tell them you can't be there." I said, "No, I need to go, I need to help. I told them I would be there, and I need to get back into the stream of life."

So we went on to Communion that night, and I'm so glad we went, because something happened that night that had never happened before or since. It was unbelievable. It was almost as if the whole congregation had rehearsed, because every worshiper, from the smallest child to the oldest adult, did the same thing. As I walked down the Communion rail serving the bread of Holy Communion, every worshiper—from the smallest child to the oldest adult—reached for the bread of Holy Communion with one hand, and with the other, they reached out and touched my hand. Now, that was in 1979, and I've got tears in my eyes right now because it was a *kairos* moment.

You know you are not supposed to talk at Holy Communion, but those wonderful people were speaking volumes to me, and here is what they were saying: "We are going to get you through this. We are going to put the heart back into you." Holy Communion had never been more holy for me than it was that night, as those wonderful people put the heart back into me in a *kairos* moment of encouragement. As I was moving down that Communion rail, serving Communion, and people were touching my hand, one after the other, time stood still. How long has it been since you had a *kairos* moment of encouragement like that?

The *Kairos* Moment of Love

Jesus had many of these, but we get so caught up in the *chronos* that we miss so many of them. I'm haunted by the question, how many wonderful *kairos* moments of love have I missed because I wasn't paying attention? Let me tell you about one I *didn't* miss, because God was with me.

I had preached one Sunday morning at the 11:00 A.M. worship service. After church was over, I was down at the Communion rail, and eleven people had joined the church. The organ was playing loudly in the background, people were visiting, and it was "happy chaos." I was trying to make the new members feel welcome and wanted, trying to take care of them, while somebody over on one side was trying to get my attention to tell me about a friend in the hospital. Somebody on the other side was trying to get my attention to introduce me to some visitors to the church. Some former members of the church who had been away had come back, and they were trying to get my attention to speak to me.

All of this was going on, when all of a sudden I felt a tug. I turned around and looked down, and it was Jeff Moore, our son—he was five years old at the time. He had come around behind the Communion rail and was tugging on me urgently. And I have to tell you that my first response was—how shall I put this—"parental." I thought to myself, *Jeff, couldn't this wait till we get in the car? I'm doing big stuff up here!* But God was with me in that moment, and he helped me to realize that there was something special and precious about that tug. So I just closed everything else out, and I dropped down on one knee to get eye-to-eye with Jeff—five years old—and here's what happened.

He was standing there—he had one hand behind his back— and when I dropped down, he just beamed! I will never forget that expression on his face. He just beamed, he was so happy that I stopped. He pulled his hand out from behind his back. He had a white paper cup with black dirt in it, and a little green plant was shooting up out of the dirt. He said, "Daddy, this is a tomato plant. God and I have been growing it in Sunday school for several weeks now. We've been studying how God makes things grow and how we can help him, and God and I have been working on this tomato plant. It's my tomato plant, but I want to give it to you and Mama this morning." Jeff said, "You're always giving *me* things, but I don't have any money to get anything for you, so I want to give you this tomato plant because I love you so much." He handed me the tomato plant, and his little arms went up around my neck, and I hugged him tightly. And in that moment, nothing else in the world mattered. In that moment of love, time stood still as we hugged each other tightly.

How long has it been since you had a *kairos* moment of love like that?

The *Kairos* Moment of Inspiration

When I was in my middle year of seminary at the Methodist Theological School in Ohio, I took a course called Pastoral Care. In addition to the academic study, they also assigned us to be interns in a nearby care facility so we could get practical experience along with our classroom work. I was assigned to be the student chaplain on the eighth floor of the Riverside Methodist Hospital in Columbus, Ohio. That was really exciting, to be the chaplain for the neurosurgery ward.

Every Thursday at 1:00 P.M., I would show up on the eighth floor and check in with the head nurse, and she would tell me about the patients: "This one had surgery two days ago." "This one is going home tomorrow." And I would go visit them. I would write up what the professors called "verbatims" and take them back to show the professor what the patient had said and what I had said. The professor would always write, "You talked too much."

One Thursday afternoon at one o'clock, the elevator doors opened, and the head nurse was standing there waiting for me. She said, "Jim, we need you today. We've never needed a minister more than we need one today. Mrs. Davis in 858 is supposed to have brain surgery at 8:00 A.M. She may not even make it off the table. There is a 50 percent chance she won't even survive the surgery, she is so ill. And she has quit on us. She won't let anyone come in the room. She won't let family come in, she won't accept any gifts or flowers, she won't answer the telephone; she is just lying there trying to die. If anybody ever needed a minister, Mrs. Davis in Room 858 needs one. Go to her."

It scared me to death. I didn't know what to say to Mrs. Davis in Room 858, who was facing surgery the next morning that she might not even survive, might not even make it off the operating table. So I started walking down toward her room, strategizing. I was young and thought I was supposed to strategize. I've learned since then that you don't do that; you just go *love* people. But I didn't know that then. I started strategizing.

Then I remembered nondirective counseling—I'd learned that in school. Nondirective counseling is when you let the other person talk and you just grunt every now and then. Or you repeat back what the person says: "I don't feel so happy today." You respond, "Oh, you don't feel happy today." And they just talk and talk, and you just "grunt" and listen and repeat, and after a while, that person just thinks you're great because you let them ventilate, and they go away happy and you're happy! So I decided, I'll use nondirective counseling on Mrs. Davis in Room 858.

I went on down the corridor toward her room, filled with confidence like a combination of John Wesley, Martin Luther, and Mother Teresa, all rolled into one. I was ready to do it! However, when I got to the door, I heard the pitter-patter of little feet behind me. I turned to see the head nurse running after me, and she said, "Oh, Jim! Wait a minute, wait a minute! I forgot the most important thing: Mrs. Davis is so critically ill that the doctors want her to be perfectly still and she is not allowed to speak."

Now, are you familiar with the word *discombobulated*? I was discombobulated! I promptly went into the room and did everything wrong. I pushed the door open too hard and it slammed against the wall. I went over and kicked the bed. (You are not supposed to do that!) I tried to talk to Mrs. Davis, and everything came out wrong. In desperation, I tried to pray and botched up the prayer. I left that room totally humiliated. I went straight to my car, and I sat in my car and felt so defeated. As if it were yesterday, I vividly remember taking my fists and hitting them on the steering wheel and screaming at God, "Why did you get me into this? I can't do this! I don't have what it takes to be a minister!"

I drove back to the seminary campus and went to see my advisor. Dr. Fred Gealy was a real smart man. I started telling him I needed to drop out of the ministry, and he said, "Jim, I'm real busy. Can you come back and see me next week?" He was buying some time.

The next Thursday, I went back to the hospital. I went up to the eighth floor of the neurosurgery ward, and I slipped into the nurses' station. I went a little early, because I knew they would be giving out the lunch trays at that time. I slipped in and looked down the list to see if Mrs. Davis had survived the surgery. I couldn't believe my eyes: There was her name! Mrs. Davis, Room 858, condition good. I was amazed!

I went down to her room and knocked on the door. Now, let me tell you, the week before, the room reeked of death—the drapes were pulled, no flowers, no cards, no gifts. But, this time, it was the total opposite. I heard somebody say cheerfully, "Come in!" I opened the door, and sunlight was streaming in, music was playing softly, and gifts and cards were all over the place. Mrs. Davis was sitting up in the bed writing thank-you notes.

I went over to her and said, "Mrs. Davis, you probably don't remember me." And she said, "Don't *remember* you? How could I ever *forget* you? You saved my life!" I turned around; I thought maybe someone else had come into the room! I said, "I don't understand. I felt so terrible—I did everything so wrong." She said, "That's just it. I felt so sorry for you!" She said, "You were so pitiful that I just wanted to hug you." She said, "I felt compassion for you, and it was the first time in months that I felt anything but self-pity; and that little spark of compassion made me want to live again." She said, "And now the doctors tell me it made all the difference."

I walked out of that room inspired! Here's why: I learned a

lesson that day that changed my life, a lesson that turned my life around. Every Sunday morning when I walk toward my pulpit, I think of Mrs. Davis. Every time I have to go with a family to tell somebody that we got bad news, I think of Mrs. Davis. Every time I sit down to talk with a couple who are having trouble in their marriage, I think of Mrs. Davis. Here's why. From that experience with Mrs. Davis that day, I learned that I don't have to be perfect. I don't even have to be good. All I have to be is faithful. Just do my best, and trust God for the rest.

If that doesn't inspire you, I don't know what would. The *kairos* moment of encouragement, the *kairos* moment of love, the *kairos* moment of inspiration. If we will just tune in to the Spirit of Christ, he has so many wonderful *kairos* moments for us!

9

Building the Ark of Confidence

Three Victories That Will Change Your Life

Scripture: Philippians 1:12-14

A friend of mine recently told me about a couple who had all of their family come for a visit. The children and the grandchildren all came, and they all stayed for ten days! Now, the couple loved having the whole family in their home, but after ten days, they were absolutely exhausted. Finally the day came for the children and grandchildren to leave. They all piled into their vehicle, but as they backed out of the drive, they accidentally ran over Grandmother's foot. She said to her husband, "Don't say a word. Just keep smiling and waving!"

Did she mean, "We don't want to make them feel badly about running over my foot," or did she mean, "We don't want to detain them or slow them down on their journey home," or did she mean, "Don't say a word! They might come back!" Whatever the case, that woman found deep down within herself the strength and resolve to go on with life, to keep on smiling and waving.

She didn't complain. She didn't fall down and wallow in self-pity. She didn't cry out for vengeance. She didn't file a lawsuit. She did not point an accusing finger. She did not say ugly things about her son-in-law who was driving the car. She just reached down within herself and found the courage and grace and fortitude to keep on standing, to keep on smiling, and to keep on waving.

This brings up a significant point, namely this: The great victories of life are won

not on the battlefields of military conflict,

not in the sports arenas of the world,

not in the marketplaces,

not in the scientific laboratories,

not even in the great expanses of space,

but rather in the souls of people like you and me. The great battles of life are won and lost inside, in the inner lives of individual people like you and me.

Now, we find a remarkable account of three such inner victories recorded early in Paul's letter to the Philippians. Paul loved these Christian friends deeply. It is interesting to note that the Philippian church was the only church from which Paul would accept a gift. The reason was, he loved them, and he knew they loved him, and he felt comfortable with them. He knew he could accept a gift from them without someone being suspicious of his motives. They were like family, and he wrote to them like a father writing to his children. And in this magnificent letter, we discover three personal victories that can change our lives, three great victories God can give to us, three great victories that build for us the ark of confidence.

Let's take a look at these.

First, We Don't Have to Be the Victims of Our Circumstances

We don't have to be victims; we can be victors! We don't have to be imprisoned or enslaved by any situation. We can, with the help of God, rise above it. Paul had made that personal breakthrough. He knew how to use his circumstances rather than be paralyzed by them. Let me show you what I mean.

If you picked up the Bible, turned to Paul's letter to the Philippians, and read it straight through with no knowledge of who wrote it (by the way, it's only four chapters long, just three or four pages, and you can read it in just a few minutes), if you read it straight through with no knowledge of the circumstances in which it was written, you would say this letter is full of joy and victory, full of strength and confidence, full of love and bigness of spirit, and you would probably have the feeling that it was written by someone who was on top of the world. It just rings with victory!

But do you know what the circumstances actually were? Let me tell you. When Paul wrote these words of joy and victory, he was in prison, in ill health, separated from his loved ones, cut off from his dream, facing death. Some scholars believe he died shortly after he wrote these magnificent words.

Pretty bad circumstances—imprisonment, ill health, separation, isolation; but Paul refused to be victimized by his external situation. There, in those deplorable circumstances, Paul used the time not to feel sorry for himself, not to throw in the towel, not to wallow in self-pity, but to write words, which later were to become treasured letters of the New Testament. He used his circumstances to stand tall and to do great things to inspire the church. "Sure I am trapped here," he said, "but it's a blessing in disguise, because people are hearing about Christ who never heard of him before." "Sure I am trapped here," he said, "but I'm going to make a victory out of this." Look at how it reads in Philippians 1:12-14.

> I want you to know, beloved, that what has happened to me has actually helped to spread the gospel, so that it has become known throughout the whole imperial guard and to everyone else that my imprisonment is for Christ; and most of the brothers and sisters, having been made confident in the Lord by my imprisonment, dare to speak the word with greater boldness and without fear.

That's the way Paul was. Whoever caught him and tried to tame him soon discovered that they had a spiritual tiger by the tail. Drag him into court, and he would turn the witness stand into a pulpit. Put him in jail, and he would convert the jailor.

Paul knew how to *use* his circumstances rather than be enslaved by them. We can do that too. Let me put it in a simple way. You see, we don't have to be *thermometers*. With God's help, we can be *thermostats*. Think about that. What does a thermometer do? It simply registers the temperature. If the temperature is warm, it registers warmth. If the temperature is cold, it registers coldness. But a thermostat *changes* the temperature, affects the temperature, influences the temperature, dictates the temperature. That is our calling as Christians—to be thermostats, not thermometers; to see every circumstance, every situation as a unique opportunity to serve the cause of Christ.

Her name is Maurine Jones. She is ninety-two years old. Her husband of seventy years recently passed away, so she decided to move into a retirement center. She waited in the lobby patiently for some time. Finally, the director of the retirement center came and told her that her room was ready. As Maurine Jones stood up and maneuvered her walker toward the elevator, the director described the way her new room looked. "I love it!" Mrs. Jones said with the enthusiasm of an eight-year-old receiving a new puppy. "But Mrs. Jones, you haven't seen the room yet," said the director. "That doesn't matter," Maurine Jones replied, "Happiness is something you decide on ahead of time. Whether I like the room or not doesn't depend on how the furniture is arranged. It all depends on how I arrange my mind, and I have already decided to love it. It's a decision I make every morning when I wake up. I can be happy or sad; I can be grateful or grumpy. Because I am a Christian, I choose to see each day as a gift from God; because I am a Christian, I choose to be happy and grateful."

This is what the apostle Paul meant later in his letter to the Philippians when he said, in effect, "I do not complain. I have learned to be content in all circumstances." (See Philippians 4:11-13.) That's the first victory. We don't have to be the victims of our circumstances. With God's help and by God's grace, we can rise above them.

Second, We Don't Have to Be the Victims of Our Pride

Some of us have problems with this. We get so caught up in being proud that we get too concerned about what people are thinking about us and whether we are receiving all the accolades we think we deserve. Some of Paul's adversaries were using his imprisonment against him personally. Back in the early days of the church, little groups were vying for power and trying to take control of the leadership of the church. So when Paul was put in prison, some of these groups saw a chance to discredit Paul, and they began to say in their preaching, "Look at this! If he were really God's man, he wouldn't be in prison."

Now, we would expect Paul to react to this, to be mad or resentful or hurt. But look how he responds. He says, in effect, "So what? It's okay. It doesn't matter what they say about me. All that matters is that the gospel is proclaimed, and in that I rejoice."

Have you heard about the newspaper editor who wanted his paper to be perfect? The newspaper's masthead carried the proud motto "The Paper That Never Makes a Mistake!" But then one day, they made a mistake, and it was a big one. A man came running into the editor's office waving the morning paper in the air and saying, "You made a mistake!" "This can't be!" said the editor. "We *never* make mistakes!" "Well, you did this time," came the man's reply. "You have printed my name in the obituary column, and I demand a correction!"

Now, a paper that makes no mistakes can't print a correction, so the editor had to come up with a creative solution. When the paper hit the streets the next morning, the man's name was printed under "New Births!" There is a sermon there somewhere, and it may be this: To live, to really live, we have to die to some things first, and one of the things we have to die to is pride. Only then can we be reborn as God's servants. If we could be

proud without being prideful,

reverent without being pompous,

bright without being snobbish,

serious without being somber,

concerned without being a crackpot,

committed without being closed-minded,

pure and good without being "holier than thou,"

then our souls would be whole, healthy, vibrant, and contagious. We don't have to be the victims of our circumstances or of our pride. With God's help, we can die to pride and be resurrected to service.

Now, here's the third breakthrough.

We Don't Have to Be the Victims of Death

Paul and all the great Christians were not afraid of death; they faced it squarely, confidently, and courageously. And so can we! If life is Christ, then death will be more of Christ, and it will not be death at all, but the entrance into a larger dimension of life with God. The great Christians have all been very sure of this. Paul says it here, in his letter to the Philippians, and elsewhere: "Rejoice in the Lord always; again I will say, Rejoice" (Philippians 4:4); "Give thanks in all circumstances; for this is the will of God in Christ Jesus for you" (1 Thessalonians 5:18). And look at Paul's remark in Philippians 1:21: "For to me, living is Christ and dying is gain."

Bishop Emerson Colaw likes to tell the story about a minister who was moving to a new assignment. His church gave him a good-bye party. The minister came into the fellowship hall early and found a floral arrangement with the message "Rest in Peace." Perplexed, he called the florist. The florist said, "You think *you've* got problems! Just think, there is a funeral somewhere in this city today with a floral spray that reads 'Good Luck in Your New Location!'"

As Christians, we don't need "good luck" when death comes, because we have Christ. We don't need a rabbit's foot, because we have God, the God who is the Lord of the living and of the dead, the God who is on both sides of the grave and is our best friend!

That's what Jesus came to show us. That's what Paul believed. *We* can believe it too, and when we do, it sets us free. It resurrects us, raises us above our circumstances, above our pride, and, yes, even above and beyond death. That's good news! The greatest news ever heard! And that's why by the grace of God and with the help of God, we can build an ark of confidence.

10
Building the Ark of Trust in God

"Surely Goodness and Mercy Shall Follow Me All the Days of My Life"

Scripture: Psalm 23

Timmy was a little five-year-old boy, an only child. His mother loved him deeply, and she was a worrier. She was concerned about his walking to school when he started kindergarten (obviously this was in a much earlier, much safer time), so she walked with him to school every morning. This worked out fine for a few days, but then Timmy told his mother that he wanted to be like the "big boys."

Timmy's mother realized that this situation was evidently embarrassing Timmy, because he protested loudly. What could be done? How could this be handled? Well, Mom (as moms can do) came up with a creative solution. She noticed that their next-door neighbor, Mrs. Goodnest, would go out each morning to take her little daughter for a walk. Timmy's mother asked Mrs. Goodnest if, while out on her morning walk, she would discreetly keep an eye on Timmy, following him to school at a distance, far enough behind him that he would not notice, but close enough to keep watch on him until he arrived safely at his school. Mrs. Goodnest said that since she was up and out early with her toddler every morning anyway, she would be glad to help out.

So the very next morning, Mrs. Goodnest and her little girl, Marcy, set out following behind Timmy as he walked to school with another five-year-old neighbor boy he knew. After about a week of this, as the little boys were walking along and chatting and kicking stones and twigs, the neighbor boy noticed that the same woman was following them every single morning. Finally, he said to Timmy, "Have you noticed that lady following us every day, pushing her baby in a stroller? Do you know her?" Timmy replied, nonchalantly, "Yeah, I know her. That's just Shirley Goodnest." "Shirley Goodnest? Who in the world is she, and why is she following us?" "Well," Timmy explained, "every night my mom makes me say the Twenty-third Psalm with my prayers, because she worries about me so much. And in it, the psalm says, 'Shirley Goodnest and Marcy shall follow me all the days of my life.' So, I guess I'll just have to get used to it!"

Well, actually, what the Twenty-third Psalm promises is not Shirley Goodnest and Marcy, but rather that God's goodness and mercy will always be with us, in every circumstance of life, in every place we walk, in every step we take, in every breath we breathe, in every valley we encounter. And, like little Timmy, we will just have to get used to it!

This is the greatest and most significant promise in all of the Bible—that God is always there for us; that God never forsakes us or deserts us; that God's goodness and mercy will follow us all the days of our lives in this world and in the world to come. *The Lord is our Shepherd*—always with us, always watching over us, always guiding us, always protecting us.

The great people of faith in every generation have always stood firmly on that promise. Look at verse 4 in Psalm 23: "Yea, though I walk through the valley of the shadow—I will fear no evil: for thou art with me" (KJV). Do you know what the psalmist is saying here? He is saying that God is always with us, but God is *especially* with us when we have to walk through the valleys of life. Let me show you what that means for us today with three thoughts.

First of All, God's Goodness and Mercy Will Be with Us When We Have to Walk Through the Valley of Despair

We can count on that! Have you heard about the tour guide who was noted for embellishing the truth? He was somewhat like the preacher whose son said of him, "Dad doesn't lie; he just remembers big!" Anyway, this tour guide was indeed "remembering big" one day as he led his group through a dark and primitive corner of Africa. They came to a region noted for its dangerous wild animals. As they walked along through the dense jungle, the tour guide showed them a place where he once had to outrun an angry cheetah. He then showed them a place where he once had to out-swim a hungry crocodile, and another place where he once had to outwit a charging rhinoceros. Finally, he showed them a place where he once had to escape from a ferocious lion. "How did you get away from that ferocious lion?" they asked. The guide looked straight up and pointed to a limb some twenty feet above his head. "Don't tell us you jumped way up there to grab that limb!" they said. The guide replied, "I missed it going up, but I caught it coming down."

So often, that happens to us spiritually. We miss God on the way up. We're so busy trying to get ahead, trying to make it to the top, that we miss God. But he is there to catch us on the way down.

You know it seems at first glance that it ought to be the other way around, that we would be most aware of God and most tuned in to him when everything is beautiful and we are on the way up, when all the breaks are going our way. But the truth is that God is never nearer to us than when we are hurting, when we are coming down, when we are filled with despair.

Often I've heard people say something like this: "This is the worst thing that's ever happened to us, but we are going to make it through this because God is with us. We can feel his presence as never before." I think there are a couple of reasons for that. For one thing, God is like a loving parent, and loving parents want so much to be with their children when their children are hurting. And also, when we are down and out, we are more open to tuning in to God, more willing to cry out for God.

The noted writer Frederick Buechner tells about a low time in his life when God broke through in an unusual way. Frederick Buechner was terribly depressed. His daughter was critically ill. He was scared and worried and weighted down with despair. He needed a word of assurance from God. He was seated one day by the roadside, worried sick thinking about his daughter, when suddenly, out of the blue, it happened—a car seemed to come from nowhere, and he got his word from God. The car had one of those personalized license plates, and the license plate bore on it a word, the one word out of the dictionary that Frederick Buechner most needed to see exactly at that moment. The word was *TRUST*.

Sitting in his car along the highway, Buechner saw God's message revealed on the license plate of a passing car. For Frederick Buechner, it was one of those life-transforming moments that cannot be explained. The burden he had felt was lifted. He did trust God again. He felt the power of hope filling his heart, and he was renewed, strengthened, reborn.

Who was the owner of the mysterious car with the license plate that said, *TRUST?* Was it a theologian trying to communicate hope to a desperate world? Was it a minister giving a one-word sermon on his license plate? Well, actually, it was the trust officer at the local bank—which reminds us once again that God works in strange and wondrous ways.

Later, that trust officer gave that license plate to Frederick Buechner. Frederick Buechner placed it on a bookshelf in his home, where to this moment it serves to remind him daily to trust in God. He says, "It is rusty around the edges and a little battered, and it is also as holy a relic as I have ever seen" (*Telling Secrets* [HarperSanFrancisco, 1991], 48).

That's number one. God's goodness and mercy are especially with us when we have to walk through the valley of despair.

Second, God's Goodness and Mercy Will Also Be with Us When We Have to Walk Through the Valley of Defeat

The story is told that back in 1850 during the California gold rush, a young man from Bavaria came to San Francisco. He was twenty years old at the time, and he brought with him some rolls of canvas. His plan was to sell the canvas to the gold miners, which they would then use for tents. Then he would use the profits from his sales to finance his own diggings for gold. However, as he headed toward the Sierra Mountains, he met up with one of the gold miners. When he told the miner his plan, the miner said, "It won't work. It's a waste of your time. Nobody will buy your canvas for tents. That's not what we need."

O Lord, help me, the young man prayed within. *I've come all this way and they don't need my canvas for tents. O Lord, what in the world am I going to do?*

Just then, he got his answer. The gold miner said, "You should have brought *pants. That's* what we need—durable pants! Pants don't wear worth a hoot up there in the diggin's. Can't get a pair strong enough."

The young man from Bavaria decided right then to turn the rolls of canvas into pants, blue pants that would survive the rigors of the gold-mining camps. He had a harness maker reinforce the pockets with copper, and the pants sold like hot cakes! By the way, the young man from Bavaria was named Levi Strauss. He called the new pants Levi's! So far, about 900 million Levi's have been sold throughout the world, and they are the only item of wearing apparel whose style has remained basically unchanged for more than 150 years.

The point is clear: God's presence with us can turn our problems into opportunities and our defeats into victories. God's goodness and mercy are with us when we have to walk through the valley of despair, and when we have to walk through the valley of defeat.

Third and Finally, Even When We Have to Walk Through the Valley of Death, We Can Count On It: God's Goodness and Mercy Will Be There as Well

Our grandson Paul is a tender spirit. He has great respect for life, and whenever one of his pets gets sick, he really feels the pain and agonizes over the situation.

When he was five years old, his goldfish got sick. Paul and everybody else in the family worked with his goldfish most of the day, trying desperately to keep the fish alive, but it was not to be. Late that Saturday afternoon, the goldfish died, and Paul was devastated. In his sorrow, he cried out, "Why did God make life so hard?"

We have all had moments like that, haven't we? His mother and father tried to help. They said, "Paul, he was just too sick, too weak. He couldn't make it, and so now he has gone to live in goldfish heaven." That helped a little, but five-year-old Paul was still in deep anguish and grief. Big sister Sarah, who was eight years old at the time, decided to help, and she said, "Paul, goldfish heaven is a wonderful place, and your fish will be very happy there." Then Sarah added what she thought would help Paul the most. She said, "Paul, in heaven you don't have to go to the doctor, and even if you did, you wouldn't have to get a shot!"

They had a funeral for the goldfish in the backyard, but Paul was still upset. So after the funeral, Sarah took it upon herself to get some construction paper and to draw for Paul her eight-year-old's interpretation of Life and Death. At the top of the page she wrote "The Circle of Life." Then, like the numbers on the face of a clock, she drew a series of small circles in the shape of a big circle.

In the first circle, she drew a picture of a baby. The second circle showed the picture of a little girl performing with a hula-hoop. In the next circle, Sarah drew her depiction of a teenage girl, and in the next, she created a picture of a young woman going to work. At the bottom of the page was a circle with a picture of a young man and woman getting married. Coming back up the page on the left-hand side was a circle showing the young couple holding a baby. And then she had the sketch of an older woman walking with a cane. The last circle showed a tombstone with these words: "Here Lies Sarah DeHondt." But then, just above the circle with the tombstone, Sarah drew a picture of an angel flying up, up, up into heaven.

Even at eight years of age, Sarah, with her "circle of life" drawing, was saying the same thing the psalmist was saying long ago. The Lord is our Shepherd, and he will always watch over us. Even though in this life we sometimes have to walk through hard valleys of despair and defeat and even death, we don't have to be afraid, because God is with us. His goodness and mercy are always with us, and when life ends for us here, then through faith in him we can go and dwell in the house of our Lord forever.

That's why we can build now the ark of trust in God.

11
Building the Ark of Christian Marriage

The Four C's of a Great Marriage

Scripture: 1 Corinthians 13:1-7

D r. Harry Emerson Fosdick once said that preaching is mass counseling. So with that thought in mind, I want to visit with you in this chapter about "The Four C's of a Great Marriage."

Why are we having so much trouble in our homes today? Why are so many marriages failing? One of the sad and painful commentaries on our modern-day world is the breakdown of family life and the breakup of so many marriages. Why is this happening, and what can we do about it?

Well, we need to understand that for a marriage to succeed and be happy and productive and fulfilling, four key things need to be happening in that relationship, and here they are.

First, There Is Communication

In a marriage, communication needs to be happening creatively on four levels: physical, social, intellectual, and spiritual. Those sound pretty obvious, but let me walk us through these.

Physical communication is the communication of "touching"—touching in all the ways that married couples want and need to touch each other, sitting close to one another, hugging one another, kissing one another, holding one another, making love with one another. Physical communication, the communication of touching, is so important to a marriage. It's not sordid or ugly. It's a sacred and beautiful gift from God, not just for the procreation of children (as miraculous and as wonderful as that is), but also for the communication and celebration of our love for one another. When you fall in love with someone, you want to be close to that person—physically close to that person.

Now, I have read in books and magazines about platonic relationships, people who get married and just love each other's minds and never touch one another. Maybe that does happen, but I think it is very rare. Most people want and need to be touched. Most people want and need physical affection. Most people want and need physical intimacy. And over the years I have noticed something. When communication breaks down in a marriage, most often the first place it "red flags" is right here. Let me show you what I mean.

A young married couple goes to a crowded party, and all is beautiful. The husband is paying a lot of attention to his wife, and they are holding hands. They are being really sweet to one another. But then some of the husband's buddies from work show up, and that "macho thing" that sometimes gets into men rears its head, and the husband begins to show off for his buddies by teasing his wife. It starts out in good fun, but he gets carried away and takes it too far, and he embarrasses her. She becomes upset, and at that moment she wants to be physically away from him, so she turns and runs out of the room. The husband thinks, *Oh, no! Why do I do that?* He is remorseful and sorry, and he runs after her to apologize. He catches up with her in the crowded living room. He touches her arm, and what does she do? She pulls away! She does not want to be touched because communication has broken down.

Now, on the other hand, when communication is right, she wants to be touched, and she wants to touch back. Physical affection is so important. Now, let me hurry to say that I am not so Freudian that I think it's the only thing that matters in a marriage, but I want to tell you that I have been around long enough to know that it's real important. It's *real* important!

Next is *social communication*. Social communication means being friends as well as lovers. It means being best friends. It means enjoying life with each other; going for a walk together; going shopping together; watching TV together; taking in a movie together; sharing meals together; talking to each other; visiting with each other; being vulnerable with each other; knowing that this person, this mate, is going to love you even though you are not perfect. It means sharing together your hopes and dreams, your victories and defeats, your strengths and weaknesses, your secrets and fears, your joys and sorrows.

Now, let me give you what I call "The Friendship Test." Imagine that you get a call this afternoon telling you that a distant relative in a distant city, a relative that you didn't even know existed, had left you thirty million dollars, tax-free. Who would be the first person or persons you would want to share this good news with? The answer to this question should tell you who your friends are.

Or turn the coin over and imagine that instead of that call this afternoon, someone calls to tell you that a person you deeply love has just been killed in a car wreck. Who would be the first person or persons you would want to share this bad news with? This tells you who your friends are.

In a good marriage, in both of those instances, the first person to come to your mind would be your mate, because your married mate should not only be your lover, but also your best friend, with whom you share the joys and sorrows of life. If the person you are married to is your best friend, then you have "heaven on earth."

Look now at *intellectual communication*. Intellectual communication is sharing the world of ideas. What matters to you? What's important to you? What is your philosophy of life? What are your priorities? What are the things that make you who you are? To talk about those things and to share your values is so important. You don't have to think exactly alike. You don't have to agree on every single thing. You don't have to have the same political party. But what you do have to have is respect for your mate's point of view. You don't have to have the same exact philosophy of life, but to have the same virtues, the same ethics, and the same morality is so crucial.

I once saw a marriage come apart at the seams because the two people involved could not respect each other's approach to life. The wife was very compassionate and tenderhearted, especially toward persons in need in our society. She had grown up in a home where, when there was a problem in the city, her parents were the first ones there to help out; and that was part of who she was, a big part of her basic make-up.

But her husband was just the opposite. He accused her of interfering in other people's lives. He didn't want to help anybody, and especially not those different from him. And that intellectual, philosophical difference tore their marriage apart. It's so important to be able to communicate physically, socially, and intellectually.

Then there is *spiritual communication*. Spiritual communication is so important. To share God, to share the Scriptures, to share the church, to share the faith, to share at least a part of your prayer life is so important.

Now, let me tell you something that is fascinating here. Normally I read *Sports Illustrated,* but somebody once gave me an issue of *Redbook* magazine that had an interesting article about love and marriage. *Redbook* had done a survey of several hundred couples, in which they had compared couples on these two levels of communication—the *spiritual* over against the *physical.* And *Redbook* magazine was honest enough to admit that they were surprised by their findings. They went into the survey expecting that those who had a strong spiritual grounding would not be very affectionate physically, and that those who were highly physically affectionate would not be very spiritual. And do you know what they found out? It was exactly the opposite! Those who were strongly spiritual enjoyed a better physical affection.

Now, if you think about that closely, it makes a lot of sense. If you don't have a strong spiritual base, then physically you tend to see the other person as an object for your gratification. But if you are spiritually grounded, then you see the other person as a child of God, a person you love so much that you want to bring pleasure to her or him. And if you have two people thinking like that at the same time, you have something special, indeed.

Think about it. What does it take to make someone a good love-mate? Well, it takes love and respect and tenderness and compassion and thoughtfulness, and that's what the spiritual life teaches us to be. The people in the survey who had a strong spiritual life, a healthy love for God, a healthy love for the church, a healthy love for other people, a healthy self-esteem—those wonderfully spiritual people had a better love life. That finding surprised *Redbook* magazine, but it shouldn't surprise us in the church, because we believe that the best sign of Christian discipleship is love—gracious, generous, self-giving love.

That's the first "C"—communication. Physical, social, intellectual, and spiritual communication.

The Second "C" Is Courtship

It is so important, so crucial, to keep the courtship alive. In many marriages in America today, the married partners share four significant roles—breadwinners, homemakers, parents (in most instances, though not all), and lovers. Now, society plays a trick on us here. During the early courtship, the engagement, the wedding, and the honeymoon, society smiles, "Isn't that sweet? Look at that great couple—so in love. Isn't that wonderful?" But then, here's the trick. After the honeymoon, society turns on us. "No! No! No! Don't be too sweet to one another. You might lose control of your life. You might get henpecked. Don't be too sweet. Rather, you just put bread on the table," society says, "that's how we are going to evaluate you. And you'd better have a nice, neat home or the neighbors and the city will march on your front door. And you'd better be good parents," society says, "or we will take your children away from you."

And by now, nobody encourages us to be good *lovers* of one another. There is so much societal pressure to succeed at bread-winning and homemaking and parenting that sometimes we use so much energy on those first three that we don't have any time or energy left over for the courtship, for the very thing that brought us together in the first place. Now, think about that. Most couples get together initially on the love and courtship level. In general, the guy does not walk into a crowded room and see this beautiful girl, and say, "Wow! Wouldn't she be a great homemaker!" That is not where he is coming from. No, he is physically attracted—or she is physically attracted—and the flirtation begins, and the courtship begins.

Here's the point: All four of the roles are important. Be great breadwinners, be great homemakers, be great parents (if you decide to and are able to have or adopt children); but in the process, don't lose each other! Keep courting, romancing, and loving each other. Make time for the courtship.

The Third "C" Is Commitment

This means going into the marriage heart and soul, committed to the love, committed to the relationship, committed to the marriage, committed to each other. The mind-set of commitment is so crucial. Let me show you why.

If you have the *trial-marriage* mind-set, the "Let's try it and see if it works" mind-set, then the first time there is a problem or some tension or some stress, your first thought is, *Well, I knew it wouldn't work, so I'll bail out now.* On the other hand, if you have the *commitment* mind-set, then when stress comes, you simply say, "Oh, a little stress here. Let's see what this is about. Let's deal with this and grow on this and learn from this." You don't think about bailing out, because you are committed. Now, let me put a footnote here. I know that some relationships become so destructive that you have no choice other than to dissolve them, but generally speaking, it is so crucial to go into the marriage with the commitment mind-set.

The first "C" is communication, the second "C" is courtship, and the third "C" is commitment.

And the Fourth "C" of a Great Marriage Is Christ and His Church

This is the most important one of all. When he was up in years, William Barclay said something that I thought was one of the greatest quotations I had ever heard outside the Bible. He said, "I'm an old man. I have lived a long time, and over the years, I have learned that there are very few things in life that really matter—but those few things matter intensely." Isn't that a great quote? "Few things in life really matter, but those few things matter intensely."

If you don't get elected second vice-president of the civic club, it's not the end of the world. It doesn't really matter that much. What are the things that matter intensely? Grace, honesty, integrity, kindness, justice, truth, morality, compassion, faith, hope, and love.

Now, wait a minute. Where have I heard all those words before? I heard them at the church. I learned them from the teaching of Jesus Christ. Even when I got them at home, they really came from Christ and the church, and those are the things that matter intensely. Those are the things that make a great marriage. Those are the things that make a great life, and they all came from Christ and his church!

One of the most beloved hymns of all time is "Blest Be the Tie That Binds." Well, Christ is the tie that binds. He is the One who unites and sustains our hearts in Christian love. He is the One who enables and empowers us to build the ark of Christian marriage.

12

Building the Ark of Purpose

What Are You Going to Do with the Rest of Your Life?

Scripture: Matthew 26:47-56

I want to begin this chapter in an unusual way—with something that was given to me by one of our church's sixth-graders. It's called an "April Fool's Aptitude Test." It's a fun test that makes a significant point—namely, that you have to really *hear* the question before you can answer it.

Here is the first question: If you take two apples from three apples, what do you have? Answer: Well, you have two! If you take two, you *have* two.

Here is the second one: Why can't a person living in Houston, Texas, be buried east of the Mississippi River? Answer: Because you don't bury living people!

Here's another one: If you have only one match, and you enter a room that has a kerosene lamp, an oil heater, and a wood-burning stove, what would you light first? Answer: The match, of course!

Now, try this one: A farmer has seventeen sheep. All but nine die. How many does he have left? Answer: Nine! They all died but nine!

Here is a sports question: In baseball, how many outs are there in an inning? Answer: Interestingly, most people say three, but the correct answer is six. Each team gets three outs, which makes six outs in an inning.

Here's one about the Bible: How many different kinds of animals did Moses take on the ark? Answer: None! *Moses* didn't take any; it was *Noah*!

How about this one: In Texas, can a man marry his widow's sister? Answer: No, because if he has a widow, he is dead!

Here is the next one: How many of your close friends were named after Abraham Lincoln? Answer: Since Abraham Lincoln died in 1865, all of your close friends would have been named *after* Lincoln [was named]!

One last question: What was our President's name in 1968? The answer is *George W. Bush*. His name is George W. Bush now, and his name was George W. Bush in 1968.

Now, on the bottom of the sixth-grader's aptitude test, the teacher had written this explanation:

> You have just taken an aptitude test for critical reading. Do you need to read more carefully? Do you need to think more carefully about what you are reading? Do you need to understand clearly what the question is really asking before you can answer it properly?

What I want us to do in this chapter is to think more carefully and more clearly about a powerful question Jesus asked in Matthew's Gospel, namely this: "Friend, why are you here?" (Matthew 26:50 RSV). It's a penetrating question; a poignant question; a personal question; a question originally addressed to Judas, but one ultimately that all of us have to answer.

Remember the scene. Jesus is in the garden of Gethsemane. The Last Supper is over. The cross looms near, and Jesus knows it. He is speaking to his disciples, trying to get them ready for what lies ahead. But then, the noise of the approaching mob catches his attention. He looks up and sees Judas leading the mob. Judas walks to Jesus and kisses the Master on the cheek (the prearranged way to identify Jesus in the dark), so that Jesus can be arrested. And then Jesus responds with this piercing question that has resounded across the ages: "Friend, why are you here?"

It's not just Judas's question; it's *your* question! And *mine*!

"Why are you here?"

"What is the meaning of your life?"

"What is your philosophy for living?"

"What is your sense of direction?"

"What is your purpose?"

"What is your faith?"

"What are you going to do with the rest of your life?"

One of the most fascinating books I have ever read is Viktor E. Frankl's *Man's Search for Meaning*. Dr. Frankl, the noted Austrian psychiatrist, was a prisoner of war for a long period of time in Nazi concentration camps. During his imprisonment, he noticed something that fascinated his analytical mind. He saw that some prisoners who came into the prison camp looking physically strong, robust, muscular, and powerful were actually weaker than some other prisoners who looked physically frail. Why was this? The difference was that those who had a sense of meaning, a direction, a purpose, a set of priorities, a vital faith— were the strongest. *Meaning* was more important than *muscles*! Those with faith fared better, could withstand more, and became an inspiration to all in the camp.

Reflecting on that discovery, Dr. Frankl wrote these marvelous words:

> We who lived in concentration camps can remember the men who walked through the huts comforting others, giving away their last piece of bread. They may have been few in number, but they offer sufficient proof that everything can be taken from a man but one thing: the last of human freedoms—to choose one's attitude in any given set of circumstances, to choose one's own way.

How important it is to know—why we are here—what our purpose is.

Some years ago, Dr. John Sutherland Bonnell was visiting with a group of young men in a college fraternity house. Dr. Bonnell turned to the chairman of the group and asked him: "What are you living for?" The student answered, "I'm going to be a pharmacist." Dr. Bonnell said, "Now, I understand that this is the way you are going to make your living, but my question is 'What are you living for?' " The young man dropped his head and answered: "Sir, I'm sorry, but I haven't thought that through yet."

Now, let me ask you something: Have *you* thought it through yet? Do you know what you are living for? Have you discovered the real priorities? Do you know how to "put first things first"? Do you really know why you are here? Do you know what you are going to do with the rest of your life? You may never have answered that question in words, but you are answering it every single day of your life by your actions and your attitudes; by what you believe; by what you stand for; by what you give your time and energy to; and, yes, by how you spend your money.

Over the years, people have answered the question "Why are you here?" in a variety of ways. Let me list a few of them.

First, Some Say, "We Are Here to Endure Life," to Persevere, to Cope, to Exist, to Stay Alive

People who answer like this see the world not as a friend, but as an enemy. They see life here as not much more than some kind of test. With this kind of attitude, life becomes drudgery, heaviness, survival, imprisonment.

One of my favorite stories fits so nicely here. Remember the first-grade teacher who walked into her classroom one morning and found little six-year-old Johnny standing up in front of the room with his tummy stuck way out? "Johnny," she asked, "why are you standing there sticking out your stomach?" "Well," said

Johnny, "I had a stomachache this morning, so I went to see the nurse, and she said if I could just stick it out till noon, maybe it would be okay!"

Unfortunately, many people go through life like that—with no sense of purpose, with no great cause, with no celebration of life. They just "stick it out till noon." They give in to boredom and apathy, to premature old age, to fear and anxiety. They do nothing exciting. They take no risks. They don't really live; they merely exist, they merely endure life, and that is so sad. I saw a graffiti message recently, which expresses it graphically. It read "Joe Smith—Died at 43, buried at 73."

What a waste that is! So, I can't be satisfied with this answer, "We are here to endure life"; can you? It doesn't ask enough of life, does it? Christ came to show us that life is not just something to be endured or escaped from. Christ came to show us that life can be beautiful, zestful, and meaningful! Christ came that we might have full, vibrant, celebratory, abundant life. Unfortunately, many people (far too many) never understand that, and in answer to the question "Why are we here?" they answer with their actions and attitudes that we are here merely to endure life.

Move with me now to a second answer.

Second, Some Say, "We Are Here to Pursue Pleasure"

There's a song that was popular some years ago, and the title sums up its message: "Enjoy Yourself (It's Later Than You Think)"! Of course, joy is a vital part of the Christian faith, and we should enjoy ourselves in the right way. The truth is that many Christians do indeed need more joy in their faith. Some do tend to get heavy and somber. And yet, Jesus (who himself had a wonderful sense of humor) said that there is more to life than selfish enjoyment alone. He was a joyful person to be sure, but he opposed the hedonistic approach of those who held to the philosophy of "Eat, drink, and be merry, for tomorrow you may die."

The truth is that the self-centered pursuit of pleasure is the surest way to miss it. The selfish pursuit of pleasure brings no lasting happiness or contentment or fulfillment. The happiest people I know are not those who are chasing after pleasure or joy as if it were about to escape them forever. The happiest people I know are those who have found meaning in life and are spending themselves in devotion to a great cause, a cause bigger than themselves.

Wilfred Grenfell, the noted missionary, once was asked to describe the hardships of being a missionary in a foreign land. After his talk, a woman approached him and said, "Oh, Dr. Grenfell, I'm so sorry you have to go through so many difficult hardships as a missionary." Grenfell responded, "Oh, my dear lady, you misunderstood me; I'm having the time of my life!"

Some say, "We are here to endure life." Others say, "We are here to pursue pleasure." Here's a third answer.

Third, Some Say, "We Are Here to Accumulate Wealth"

When our son Jeff was five years old, he did something in church one Sunday morning that we have chuckled about for years. It was during the first hymn. The young minister standing next to me on the platform began laughing and said to me, "Look at your son!" I looked out and saw, on the first pew, five-year-old Jeff Moore holding his hymnal out rather angelically in front of him, with two half-dollars squeezed into his eye sockets! They were held in place by a marvelous, mischievous squint!

As I saw him there, I thought to myself two things—first, *Where did he get two half-dollars,* and then too, I thought, *Isn't that a great parable for life!* He couldn't see the hymnal. He was just holding it out in front of him. He couldn't see anything because of the half-dollars in his eyes. It happens that way with some people; money and possessions become blinders! They give all their energy and time and effort to making money, to accumulating wealth, and they become blind to everything else.

Someone once asked the great actor Henry Bosworth, "What is the greatest thing that a person can have?" He answered, "That's easy. It isn't money, because you can't hold on to it. It isn't fame, because they will cheer you one minute and sneer you the next. But if you can have peace in your heart, that is the thing that really matters when all else is done." It's important to make a living. But it's far more important to make a life! It's good to have money and the things money can buy, but that is not the most important thing we can give our families.

Patrick Henry closed his will with these words: "I have now disposed of all my property to my family. There is one more thing I wish I could have given them, and that is the Christian religion. ...If they had that, and I had not given them one shilling, they would be rich, and if they had not that, and I had given them all the world, they would be poor" (Dyer, *Our Only Hope*).

"Why are we here?" It's not enough just to endure life. It's not enough just to pursue pleasure. It's not enough just to accumulate wealth.

There is another answer. Jesus gives it to us.

Jesus Christ Says, "We Are Here to Love God and to Love People"

Jesus said that the greatest commandment (the ultimate answer) is to "love the Lord your God with all your heart, and with all your soul, and with all your mind," and a second commandment is to "love your neighbor as yourself" (Matthew 22:37-39). Do this, he said, and you will really live! Someone once said, "Life is God's gift to us, and how we use it is our gift to God."

A few years ago, some of our church's Sunday school children were asked to complete two sentences: "I love my mom because..." and "I love my dad because..." Their responses were beautiful, poignant, funny, and perceptive. Here's a quick sampling. (Look for the common thread that runs through them.)

A six-year-old boy said, "I love my mom because she told me about God, and I love my dad because he told me right from wrong."

A nine-year-old boy wrote, "I love my mom because she provides a home for me, but most importantly she provides love. And I love my dad because he provides many fun stuff for me."

A four-year-old girl said, "I love my mom because she is nice, and I love my dad because he keeps me from doing bad things."

And look at this one. A nine-year-old girl wrote, " I love my mom because she is very nice and she helps me a lot. Also, because she always brings back "souvaneers" from different places. And I love my dad because he lets me play with him, and because he can be very flexible—sometimes!"

A three-year-old girl said, "I love my mom because she is happy! And I love my dad because he is old!"

Another three-year-old girl said, "I love my mom because she takes me to Sunday school, and I love my dad because he gave me an Easter costume."

A fifth-grade girl, age eleven, wrote, "I love my mom because she's cool, loving, gentle, and kind, and is understanding. She gives me wise advice. She is good at last-minute projects. And I love my dad because he makes the best of every situation, with a smile. When I'm upset, he puts on a smile and uses a funny voice."

A six-year-old boy said, "I love my mom because she grosses out when I show her my loose tooth. She is funny. And I love my dad because he calls me Buddy."

This final one sums it all up. A nine-year-old boy wrote this: "I love my mom because she keeps me on the right path. She feeds me and helps me with my homework. She is a great person in my life. And I love my dad because he taught me how to fish and hunt and play baseball. He loves me and cares for me. He is a great person in my life."

Aren't those great? And, of course, the common thread that links them together is the fact that these children are learning at home and at church the greatest lesson in life—how to love God and how to love people. That's what it's all about.

Many years ago, there was a young man who came from a very well-to-do family, who would not have had to work a day in his life. But he chose to work for God. He took a vow of poverty. He became a priest and founded a religious order. He became known and respected all over the world because of his love for God, and God's world, and all of God's creatures and animals. He was a man of justice and compassion and humility. His name was Francis of Assisi. He wrote a prayer that underscores for us how to put first things first, and the words of this magnificent prayer remind us beautifully of why we are here. Here are those powerful words:

Lord make me an instrument of your peace,
Where there is hatred let me sow love;
Where there is injury, pardon;
Where there is doubt, faith;
Where there is despair, hope;
Where there is darkness, light;
and Where there is sadness, joy.
O Divine Master, grant that I may not so much seek to be consoled as to console;
to be understood as to understand; to be loved as to love;
for it is in giving that we receive;
it is in pardoning that we are pardoned and it is in dying that we are born to eternal life.

13
Building the Ark of Freedom

Why Do We Wait for Permission?

Scripture: Luke 13:10-17

Have you ever noticed that many people go through life just waiting around, waiting for permission to really live?

Indeed, many people are frustrated because they have never really outgrown the security of being controlled by someone else. They don't feel that they have permission to take charge of their own lives, so they wait around for someone else out there to give them permission—permission to live, to change something in their life that ought to be changed, to do something creative, to take charge of their lives.

In Luke 13, we see a vivid example of this. Jesus sees a woman in the synagogue who has been bent double by some spiritual burden. She has been unable to stand up straight for over eighteen years. Jesus has compassion for her, and he gives her permission to put the problem behind her. "You are rid of your trouble," Jesus says to her, and she straightens up and praises God.

That's wonderful, isn't it? But, let me ask you something. Why did she have to wait eighteen years? Why didn't someone give her permission earlier to throw off this burden? Why didn't she give herself permission? Why did she resign herself to this awful plight? And why do we? Why do we wait around for permission to throw off these burdens that crush us?

Bent double, this woman was, by a "spirit" that had gripped her and shackled her for almost twenty years. For all that time, she had not been able to stand up straight because she was so ashamed, so guilt-ridden, so worn-down, so burdened, so humiliated. Then Jesus happened along, and, perceptive as he was, he saw straight to the core of her problem. He told her to put it behind her. In effect, he gave her permission to straighten up, and she did!

Don't miss something very important in this story—namely, that the woman's problem was a spiritual one. You remember, of course, that in many of the healing miracles in Jesus' ministry, the focus is on something physical—blindness or paralysis or illness—some physical disease or disability.

In this story, though, the woman is bent double because of something gone wrong spiritually. The original Greek text calls it a "spirit of weakness."

Don't you wish we could know the rest of the story? Don't you wish the writer had given us a bit more information, a few more details?

Had she been involved in some public scandal that had left her stooped in shame?

Had she been caught in some sordid sin that had left her doubled over in humiliation?

Had she done something so terrible that people around her steered clear for fear of guilt by association?

Had her past been so disgraceful that it had burdened her to the point that she was bent down with guilt?

We just don't know. The Scriptures don't tell us. They give us only the bottom line: namely, that when Jesus said to her, "You are set free from your ailment," that was all she needed to unbend. When he assured her that she was forgiven, it set her free from the awful burden that had been pushing her down for so many years.

Jesus' saying it miraculously made it feel all right for her to stand tall. Jesus' saying it miraculously made it feel all right for her to put it behind her and to accept God's forgiveness. Jesus' saying it miraculously made it all right to forgive herself and to pick up the pieces of her life and start all over again.

End of story? Everyone lives happily ever after? No, not quite! Instead, the leader of the synagogue was angry, indignant, and aggravated because Jesus had healed the woman on the sabbath.

"Now see here!" the leader says. "You have broken the law. Look what you have done. You have healed someone on the sabbath day; you have forgiven someone on this holy day; you have given someone a new lease on life on the Lord's Day. This is unheard of—unspeakable! The people have six days to find healing. Why did you have to go and help this woman on the sabbath?"

Jesus answers, in effect, "Look what has happened to us. Can't you see it? Are we perfectly willing to help an animal on the sabbath, but not a person? Is it okay to bring comfort to an ox or a donkey on the sabbath, but not to a human being? How ridiculous! The church is here to *help* the people, not to abuse them. The church is here to bring healing and forgiveness to the people, not to lay more guilt on them. Is it not fitting to help this woman who has been burdened for eighteen years? Eighteen years is long enough! She shouldn't have to wait another day!" Then the people rejoiced at what Jesus had said and for what he had done.

Isn't that a great story? It sounds (at first hearing) like an ancient story, far removed from where we are in our lives today. But look closer, and notice "the permission syndrome"!

The woman was resigned to her plight until Jesus came along—until Jesus came and gave her permission to be okay, permission to start over, permission to live again. Now, that "permission problem" is still with us! Crazy as it may sound, it is a lot more common than we may think. Look at these red-flag statements:

"We never did it that way before."

"No one will tell me what to do."

"I want to change my life, but nobody will really tell me how to change it."

"I can't do that."

"There is no way I can take that risk because I might fail."

"I want to go, but I'm not sure I should."

"How could I ever be forgiven for what I've done?"

So we wait for permission. We wait for somebody, some law, some authority, some thing, some rationale from outside, some fortunate change in circumstances that will say to us that it's okay, and that we are free to do or to move or to be that which we, for some strange reason, do not feel we have permission to do or be on our own. We wait for permission to *live*.

Now, with this in mind, let me remind you that part of the good news of Christ is that he sets us free—unshackles us, relieves us of our burdens, forgives us, encourages us, challenges us, inspires us, motivates us, saves us. In other words, he gives us permission to live—to really *live*!

Let me show you what I mean, for example.

Christ Gives Us Permission to Stand Tall for What Is Right

The woman in Luke 13 had been bent over for eighteen years. For eighteen years, no one had helped her. The people didn't realize that they had permission. They didn't realize that this is why the church exists. They were waiting for someone else to do it.

Some years ago, when I finished seminary and was serving one of my first churches, I was ready to set the world on fire—but for a short period, I became downhearted and disillusioned. The little church I was sent to had never had a full-time pastor before, and they were doing so many things wrong. I became saddened by the poor plight of this church, and in despair, one gray day when I was feeling especially blue, I sat down and wrote a letter to one of my seminary professors, Dr. Fred Gealy.

In that letter, I assessed the situation, and I listed all the problems in that little church. The letter sounded pretty bleak as I described all the troubles and problems in my church.

In a few days, Dr. Gealy's response came in the mail. It was a nice letter. He told about the weather, the spring flowers on campus, a couple of new professors, and some dreams of his for the seminary. He then spoke of Mrs. Gealy's health and sent his love to our family, and he concluded the body of the letter.

At the bottom was a postscript, a P.S. that I will never forget. It read, "P.S. By the way, Jim, with regard to the problems in your church—what's a pastor for???"

Dr. Gealy was gently nudging me and reminding me that I had permission to change those things. I had permission to teach the people the right way to do things. I had permission to be a pastor, a spiritual leader. I had permission to stand tall for what is right. In effect, he was saying, "Jim, why don't you quit assessing things and get to *doing* something!"

I have thought of that P.S. often. Some years later, we had a youth minister on the staff of a church I was serving who kept assessing the youth department instead of feeling permission to change it. "These youth are not interested," he would say. "They don't know what to do," he would say. "They don't feel committed," he would say. Then one day, we had to say to him, "What's a youth minister for?" We had to remind him that he had permission to do something about the situation, that he had permission to change it, that he had permission to stand tall for what is right.

That's what Jesus did in Luke 13. He *became* the church. He changed a bad situation. He brought forgiveness and healing and life and peace to a troubled soul, and in so doing, he gave us permission to be agents of creative change. He stood tall for what was right. And *we* have permission to do that too!

Christ Gives Us Permission to Forgive

Jesus introduced grace and mercy and forgiveness into the law in a fresh, new way. The law of the day back then was the law of retribution: in other words, if you do something bad to me, then I must do the exact same bad thing back to you, so that justice can be served. Also, there was another distorted notion running rampant. It was believed that if persons were sick or afflicted, they had done something to bring God's judgment on themselves. The people didn't want to tamper with God's judgment, so they shunned the troubled persons.

In other words—and here is the point—in the time of Jesus, the commonly accepted understanding was: "I do not have the choice to forgive. I must repay you, an eye for an eye and a tooth for a tooth, and I must let God's justice and judgment be served."

But then Jesus came, and he didn't shun them. He loved them and granted permission to forgive. Remember how he was criticized. "Wait a minute," the people said, "only God can forgive!" But Jesus said, "No! You can forgive! We all can forgive! In fact, we *ought* to forgive. We ought to imitate the forgiving spirit of God in all that we do."

Marshall Steele told a great story about this when he was pastor at Highland Park Church in Dallas. A country doctor inspected the water on a farm. He found one pond with water that was unsafe to drink. He called all the workhands together and told them, "Do not drink from this pond. The water is poisonous!" He also put a big sign in the pond that read *Danger! Unsafe water! Do not drink!*

The very next day, the farmer's son got hot while working. He ignored the doctor's warning. He ignored the doctor's sign. He drank from the condemned pond. He became deathly ill in the night. They called the doctor and told him what happened. What did the doctor do? Did he say, "I told you so"? Did he say, "Don't blame me"? Did he fuss at the farmer's son? Did he turn his back on him? Did he refuse to come? No! He came and sat up all night with that sick young man and saved his life. Do you know why? Because the doctor knew that he had permission to forgive. He had learned that from the Great Physician.

One other quick thought here. We also have permission to forgive *ourselves*. We all make mistakes, but we can learn from our mistakes and grow from them and forgive ourselves, and, with the help of God, make a comeback.

In this great story in Luke 13, Jesus reminds us that (1) we have permission to stand tall for what is right, and (2) we have permission to forgive.

Christ Gives Us Permission to Start Over Again, to Bounce Back, to Make a Comeback, to Pick Up the Pieces of Our Lives and Make a New Start

Simon Peter realized this, but Judas didn't, and that was the glory of Peter's life and the tragedy of Judas's life. The woman in Luke 13 was resigned to her burdened state, but Jesus came into her life and gave her permission to start over again.

Isn't it interesting to note how we today place such a great emphasis on *starting out* on something? We make a big deal over starting out in a new position or a new marriage or a new career or a new house. There is something very exciting about starting out on those first steps of a new journey.

However, the truth is, some of life's greatest moments come not when we start out, but when we start over. Over the years, I have seen great excitement in the eyes of people who are making a new start with their lives.

When I was in college, one of my classmates was a sixty-year-old woman. Earlier, she had dropped out of college to get married and have a family, and then forty years later, she was back on campus, thrilled to have the opportunity to start over and to get her college education. With her children grown and her husband supportive, she was starting over again. A nervous, thrilled, grateful sixty-year-old sophomore—what a beautiful sight!

Some years ago, a middle-aged man came to my office. He had been highly successful in the business world, but then he felt God tugging at his heart and calling him into the ministry. He turned away from a lucrative salary and enrolled in seminary. He was so excited. He couldn't wait to get to class to learn everything he could learn, so he could become the minister God was calling him to be. He was thrilled beyond words for the chance to start over.

This is without question one of the greatest teachings of Christianity—that it is never too late to start over. This is the "good news" of our faith. God has a new beginning, a new chance, a new start, a new life for us. God offers us new opportunities and then gives us the strength to grab hold of them and celebrate them. No matter what has happened in the past, no matter how many years we have under our belts, no matter how many bad mistakes we may have made along the way, it is never too late to start over again. Why is this? Because our God is the God of Resurrection who can turn sorrow into joy, problems into opportunities, defeats into victories, death into life.

And also because he gives us permission to live, to really live! He gives us permission to stand tall for what is right, and permission to forgive one another. He gives us permission, when we stumble and fall, to get up and start all over again.

14

Building the Ark of Perseverance

Why Do People Drop Out?

Scripture: 2 Timothy 4:6-18

Someone has called this "The Age of the Dropout"—
and with good reason! We see young people dropping
out of school. We see couples dropping out of their
marriage commitment. We see teenagers dropping out
on their families, running away from home, taking to
the streets. And we see well-trained professional people suddenly dropping out of their careers.

For ages now, we have read about or heard about runaway
fathers, men who (for whatever reasons) choose to desert their
families. But in recent years (in the last decade or so), we have
seen a new sociological phenomenon—"the Dropout Mom,"
mothers who (pressed to the breaking point) pack up, leave
a note, and drop out on their responsibilities as wives and
mothers.

Then, too, we see people dropping out on their faith commitment and their church. In the church, we have traditionally
called this "back-sliding," but in contemporary language we call
these folk "church dropouts." Now, why does this happen? Why
do people drop out in such astonishing numbers today? And in
particular, why do people drop out of the church? Let me list
some thoughts. I'm sure you will think of others.

First, Some People Drop Out Because They Get Stressed Out

I think at least a part of the answer is that we live in a stress-ful world, and many people have not learned how to handle stress creatively. When things go wrong, when tensions rise, when problems mount, when stress comes, the temptation is to drop out, to run away, to go and hide. Some people do just that. Rather than work through the problem and learn from it and grow on it, they drop out! They quit! They throw in the towel!

A few months ago, I was asked to lead a workshop called "How to Deal with Stress" at a regional teachers' convention. When I checked in, the registrar showed me a listing of all the different workshop choices for the teachers. It was a long and impressive list. The registrar said, "You will have the largest group in your workshop." "Oh, really?" I responded. Then she added, "That's right, but before you get the big head, you need to know that it's not *you;* it's your *subject.*" She went on to say, "All we have to do to get the crowd out is put the word *stress* or the word *cope* in the title, and they come running for help."

The point is obvious. Life can be tough, no question about it. And people do need help in the struggle. In the movie *Oh, God! Book II,* George Burns plays the part of God. A little girl asks him why bad things happen. George Burns thoughtfully considers her question, and then he replies, "That's the way the system works [in this world]. Have you ever seen an up without a down? A front without a back? A top without a bottom? You can't have one without the other. I discovered that if I take away sad, then I take away happy, too. They go together." Then, with a smile, he adds, "If somebody has a better idea, I hope they put it in the suggestion box."

Life is difficult and stressful, and occasionally it can be very discouraging. And sometimes we want to just give up and run away from it all. That's actually what happened with one of the top leaders of the early church. His name was Demas. He was an important Christian missionary. For a while, Demas was the apostle Paul's right-hand man. He worked with Paul, traveled with him, even spent some time in prison with him. But something went wrong. Something happened to Demas, and the final word we have on him is one of the most poignant verses of Scripture in all of the New Testament. The apostle Paul is speaking, and he says: "Demas has forsaken me! In love with the present age, Demas has forsaken me" (2 Timothy 4:10, paraphrased). In other words, Demas was a dropout. That's the last report we have on him. He simply dropped out on what turned out to be the greatest enterprise in human history.

Recently, I visited a good friend who has been doing battle with a long-term illness for many months. He is making progress now, but it is so slow, so tedious, so painful, so hard. I was impressed by two posters stuck on the wall directly in front of his hospital bed, so that he could see them constantly. One of them was the picture of a little kitten hanging precariously from a tree limb by his two front paws, with a look of desperation on his face. The caption underneath read, "Hang in There!" The other poster, right next to it, was simply four words in bright red letters: "Keep On Keeping On!"

Well, the truth is, that isn't always easy. Sometimes it is very difficult to "Hang in There" and to "Keep On Keeping On." There is, indeed, sometimes a strong temptation to turn back, to give in, to drop out, and that weighs very heavily upon us. At times like those, I think it's helpful to remember Demas, and to remember what he missed by dropping out. Don't you wonder what was in Demas's mind that day when he went "over the hill"? What was it that caused him to desert Paul and the church? Maybe it was the stress. Some people do drop out because they get stressed out.

Second, Others Drop Out Because They Get Disagreed With

These people have an idea and they express it, but someone disagrees with them, and they feel personally rejected, they feel threatened, they feel that they have been attacked. They have not learned that "it's okay to disagree; just don't be disagreeable about it."

In his book *Letters and Papers from Prison* (revised edition, New York: Macmillan, 1967), Dietrich Bonhoeffer reflects on his experiences in the Holocaust death camps. He saw something there that was fascinating to him. He said, "I notice repeatedly here how few there are who can harbor conflicting emotions at the same time" (page 163).

In that awful, confining, dehumanizing, debilitating experience, there was very little contrast of feelings: Everyone was scared, everyone was hungry, everyone was tired, everyone wanted to be free. There is very little contrast of feelings in a prison camp.

On the other hand, in a healthy church, there is a constant flow of ideas. There are contrasts, discussions, dialogues, airings of views, and differences of opinion—and that is good. It's healthy. How boring it would be if we all saw everything exactly the same. As someone once expressed it, "Put thirteen Methodists in a room, and you have nineteen opinions!"

But there are some people who have never learned how to disagree without being disagreeable. They cannot handle disagreement. They don't understand the Christian way of being able to grapple with issues and still love people, even those people who see things differently. So when these folk are involved in a disagreement (especially if they don't get their way), they drop out. Is it possible that this was Demas's problem? Maybe he and Paul had a disagreement. Some people do drop out because they get stressed out. Others drop out when they get disagreed with.

Third, Still Others Drop Out Because They Feel Left Out

Dr. D. L. Dykes once told of visiting a civic luncheon to hear a man talk about the art of leadership. The man began his speech in an interesting way. He asked for three volunteers from the audience. He put them in a circle, with one man on his right, one directly in front of him and one to his left. Then the leader reached in his pocket and pulled out a tennis ball and said, "Let's play catch." He tossed it to the man on his right who then threw it to the man in the middle, who pitched it to the man on the left and then back to the leader. Round the circle it went several times.

But then the leader took the ball, walked over, and whispered something to the man in the middle and the one on the left. Then the leader came back to his position, and this time he bypassed the man on the right. He threw it directly across to the man in front of him, and around it went. They continued to bypass the man on the right.

What do you think happened next? The man on the right, the one being left out, looked embarrassed, and quietly he walked back to his seat and sat down. He dropped out.

The leader had made his point. He went to the microphone and said, "See what happens when you leave somebody out? They drop out on you! They quit on you!" And he went on to say, "I'll tell you something else, if you let him sit there long enough, he will not only quit on you, but he will also begin to criticize the way the others are throwing the ball!"

How true that is! Some people drop out because they feel left out. Maybe that's what happened to Demas. Maybe he felt left out. Maybe he felt that Paul was not giving him enough to do or that Paul was not sharing the limelight. Maybe he was jealous. Maybe he resented Paul for giving so much attention to Timothy. Maybe he felt left out, and so he dropped out. But it doesn't have to be that way, because God has shown us with a cross that we are loved, we are accepted, we are valued, and we are included.

Some drop out because they get stressed out. Others drop out because they get disagreed with. Still others drop out because they feel left out.

Fourth and Finally, Some People Drop Out Because They Feel Overwhelmed

Some years ago, the treasurer of the New York Philharmonic Society came to make his annual pitch to the noted philanthropist Andrew Carnegie. This was one of Carnegie's favorite charities, and, as he had done in the past, he asked what was the total indebtedness. When he was told $60,000, he sat down and began to write a check to cover the entire deficit. But suddenly, Andrew Carnegie stopped and said, "Wait a minute! Surely there must be other music lovers in this city who could help out. Why don't you raise half this amount, and then come back to me for the other half?" Thus was created what we now call the "matching grant."

The very next day, the treasurer came back beaming and told Carnegie that he had already raised the $30,000 and would like to get Mr. Carnegie's check now. Andrew Carnegie was immensely pleased at this show of enterprise and immediately handed it over. But he was curious. "Who, may I ask, contributed the other half?" The treasurer answered, "Mrs. Carnegie!" (Peter Hay, *The Book of Business Anecdotes,* N.Y. Facts on File Publications, 1988).

Now, that is a light treatment of a very serious subject. Sometimes we feel as though we are having to do it all. That's one of the signs of "burnout." Maybe this happened to Demas. After all, being a leader in the early church was no easy task. It was tough. It was awesome. It was scary. It was lonely. And I'm sure there were some days when it may have seemed quite hopeless. They had so many things against them, so many hardships, and so much persecution. Demas may well have cried out, "What's the use? This is impossible! Where is God anyway? Why doesn't he help us more?" And then, overwhelmed by it all, he may have thrown his hands up and dropped out.

Some people do that. Like Demas, they make the mistake of not realizing that God is going to win in the end. Ultimately,

God and his truth and righteousness will win. No matter how dark it may seem, no matter how overwhelming it may sometimes feel, no matter how many death dirges we hear, no matter how many cries of despair are issued, the church survives; it lives on; it endures.

The church is not dead, and it is not dying, because the church is of God, and it will endure to the end of time. God will win in the end, and the good news of our faith is that God chooses to share the victory with you and me. So please, please don't drop out on God, and don't drop out on the church. "Hang in There," and "Keep On Keeping On," and with the help of God, you can build the ark of perseverance.

15
Building the Ark of Sacrificial Love

Continuing the Ministry of Christ's Love

Scripture: Mark 11:1-10; Philippians 2:1-11

Have you heard the beautiful legend called "The Legend of Bamboo"?

Once upon a time, there was an exquisite garden in the heart of a great kingdom. Of all the plants in the garden, the most beautiful (and the most beloved) to the master of the garden was the splendid and noble Bamboo. Each year, Bamboo grew in beauty and stature, and he was very conscious of his master's love.

One day the master came to the garden and looked at Bamboo. In passion and love, Bamboo bowed his head to the ground in joyful greeting. The master spoke: "Bamboo, I have need of you. I want to use you for a special purpose. Of all the plants in my garden, it's a service only you can perform." Bamboo flung his head to the sky in utter delight. He was thrilled, and he said, "O Master, I am ready. Use me as you will."

But then, the master's voice was grave and serious. "Bamboo, to accomplish this, you will have to be cut down." At first, this was hard for Bamboo to understand. "If I am the master's favorite plant in the garden, then why must I be cut down? Use me as you will, O Master, but do I have to be cut down?" "O my beloved Bamboo," the master said, "If you are not cut down, you cannot be used."

The garden grew very still and quiet. All the other plants watched and listened intently for Bamboo's response. Bamboo slowly bent his glorious head and with a deep and humble bow, he said, "O Master, let us do what is needed. If I cannot be used unless I am cut down, then here I am; let the cutting begin." The master said, "Your leaves and branches must be cut as well." In obedience, Bamboo answered, "I am your servant; I will do what I must."

Then the master said: "Bamboo, you must be divided in two." Humbly, Bamboo yielded himself to be cut and divided. Bamboo was cut down. His branches were taken off. His leaves were stripped away. He was divided in two. Then he was carried to a spring of fresh water, sparkling, clean water, in the midst of a dry field. The master put one end of broken Bamboo into the spring, and the other end into the water channel in his field. Then the clear, sparkling water raced joyously down the channel of Bamboo's broken body into the waiting parched fields.

Within a short time, a miracle began to happen: tiny shoots of rice began to grow. Nourished by the water brought by Bamboo, the rice grew and grew and grew, and in time there was a great harvest. And on that day, Bamboo, once so glorious in his stately beauty, was yet even more glorious in his brokenness and humility. For in his beauty, he was life abundant, but in his brokenness, he became a channel of abundant life to his master's world.

Now, this is a timely parable for us today because in this poignant parable we have the essence of the Christ event. This is what the apostle Paul was trying to tell the world about his Savior Jesus Christ, and about the power of his sacrificial love. Jesus was cut down, but then he was lifted up, and he became the channel of abundant life. Remember how Paul put it:

Jesus "emptied himself, taking the form of a servant" (Philippians 2:7 RSV).

He "gave himself for us" (Titus 2:14).

"He humbled himself" (Philippians 2:8).

He "became obedient to the point of death" (Philippians 2:8).

He died for us on a cross. "Therefore God also highly exalted him / and gave him the name / that is above every name, / so that at the name of Jesus / every knee should bend / ... and every tongue should confess / that Jesus Christ is Lord" (Philippians 2:9-11).

This is the message of the Bible. This is the message of the Christian faith. This is the message of sacrificial love. On Palm Sunday, our Lord entered the Holy City on a donkey (in Mark 11, referred to as a "colt") as the Prince of Peace, the King of kings, the Good Shepherd who came to lay down his life for his sheep. Then on the following Thursday night (in the upper room), Jesus broke the bread and offered the cup and said to the disciples, "Do this in remembrance of me" (Luke 22:19). What does that mean? Do *what* in remembrance of him? Celebrate Holy Communion? For sure Jesus meant this, but there is more here than just that. He also meant:

Now you live in this spirit of the broken body and the shed blood as a memorial to me.

Now you take up this torch of sacrificial love as a memorial to me.

You want to honor me? Then be humble servants.

You give yourself away for my sake.

You reach out to others in self-giving love. Nothing could honor me more or please me more than to see you sacrificing for others.

Sacrificial love—that's what it's all about. You live in that spirit. Do this in remembrance of me!

In his youth, Count Nikolaus von Zinzendorf was a very devoted Christian. He loved the church and practiced his faith daily. But his parents died when he was still young, and the young count became quite promiscuous. He turned to all kinds of vices and sinful ways, and he completely turned his back on the things of faith that he once had loved. His parents had left him in the care of an old coachman who had been like a member of the family for many years, and the older man was heartbroken over the young count's shortcomings and evil ways.

One day as they were driving up to the city, the old coachman told Count Nikolaus that he wanted to take him to see a special painting at the art gallery. Count Nikolaus was not particularly interested, but to humor his friend, he agreed to go. When they arrived in the city, they went at once to the art gallery. They walked down a long corridor until they came to a great painting at the end of the hallway. The painting covered the entire wall. The old coachman pointed it out and asked the young man to look at it.

It was a painting of Jesus hanging on the cross. Count Nikolaus von Zinzendorf studied the painting very carefully. He followed every line out to the end of the canvas. He looked at the nailprints in the hands and feet. He saw the blood trickling down the face of the Master, set flowing by a cruel crown of thorns. He saw the mingled look of pity and compassion in Jesus' eyes. The young man stood there and studied the painting for a long time. Finally, his eyes fell on the legend at the bottom of the painting. It said simply: "All this I did for Thee. What hast Thou done for me?"

That was the turning point in the life of Count Nikolaus von Zinzendorf. He returned to the Christian faith and became a great supporter of the church, and a great exponent of the Christian lifestyle. He realized that day that Christ has given his all for us, and that our calling now is to take up the torch of Christ's sacrificial love, to imitate Christ's gracious ways, and to live in that self-giving spirit.

Now, let me be more specific and bring this closer to home. Let's break this down a bit and look together at some of the special ingredients in sacrificial love.

First of All, Sacrificial Love Is Generous

Sacrificial love is big-hearted and big-spirited. It is gracious, thoughtful, kind, and giving. Generosity is one of the key elements in sacrificial love.

Some years ago, the famous Argentine golfer Roberto

DeVincenzo won a major golf tournament. He was given a large check (in the hundreds of thousands of dollars) for his winnings. After the ceremonies, Roberto DeVincenzo was walking toward his car when he met a somber, sad-eyed young woman. Slowly, she walked up to him and said, "It's a happy day for you, but a sad day for me. I have just come from the hospital. They tell me my baby daughter has cancer, and if she doesn't have surgery right away, she will not live out the month. I don't know what to do. I have no money and no insurance."

Before she could say another word, Roberto DeVincenzo took out a pen, endorsed his winning check, and put it in the woman's hand, urging her to "take the money and do what's best for your baby." Some of the golfer's friends saw what happened, and they became suspicious. They checked into the story and found that it was all a hoax. The woman had no sick baby. She had tricked Roberto DeVincenzo out of hundreds of thousands of dollars.

DeVincenzo's friends came back to him and said: "Roberto, we have terrible news. The young woman was a phony. It was a hoax. She tricked you out of your winnings." On hearing this, Roberto DeVincenzo said, "You mean there is no sick baby? There is no baby girl with cancer? Why, that's the best news I've heard all week!" That kind of unselfish, generous spirit is the stuff sacrificial love is made of.

Now, where did Roberto DeVincenzo get that spirit of generosity? He got it from Jesus Christ! Even if he didn't realize where it came from, it came from Jesus Christ, because in Christ, sacrificial love was introduced dramatically into the world as never before. Of course, there are noble examples of sacrificial love in the Old Testament. We see it in Abraham, in Moses, in David, in Hosea. But nowhere do we see it more powerfully than in the gracious and generous gift of Jesus Christ to the world.

The Gospel of John puts it like this: "For God," in his amazing generosity, "so loved the world that he gave his only Son, that whoever believes in him should not perish but have eternal life" (John 3:16 RSV).

Second, Sacrificial Love Is Unconditional

This is *agape*—uncalculated goodwill for all people, unselfish love, love in all circumstances, love with no reservation, unfettered love, love with no conditions, love with no strings attached. It is unwavering, unshakable, unflinching love.

More than anything, this is what Jesus came to teach us: how to love unconditionally. In Jesus, we see what God is like. In him, God is saying, "Look! This is how I love all of you—my love for you is unconditional. Nothing you can do will stop me from loving you! You can betray me, deny me, taunt me, beat me, curse me, spit on me, nail me to a cross, and I will keep on loving you. I love you like that—unconditionally!"

And don't miss this: *That* is the way God wants us to love *one another*. You see, I can't say, "I will love you if you are good to me" or "I will love you if you love me back." I can't say that and live in the spirit of Jesus Christ. I can live in his spirit only by loving unconditionally, expecting nothing in return, loving unselfishly.

Robert E. Lee was once asked his opinion of a certain man. General Lee responded, "He is a fine and able man, and I commend him to you highly!"

"But, General," the questioner protested, "don't you know the terrible things this man says about you?"

"Yes," Lee answered, "I know, but you didn't ask how he felt about me. You asked what I think of him, and I think he is a fine and able man, and I commend him to you highly."

That is unconditional love, and that is our calling as Christian disciples.

Sacrificial love is generous, and it is unconditional.

Third and Finally, Sacrificial Love Is Self-Giving

Some years ago, a man called his minister. The man's wife had just given birth to a baby boy. The baby was fine, except for one thing: He had no right ear. The auditory opening was there, and all the inner ear parts were there, but there was no outer ear. The doctors assured the parents that eventually transplant surgery could be performed, but they would have to wait till the boy was fully grown, and of course, a donor would have to be found.

Years passed, and the little boy grew up with no right ear. Over the years, he was teased and called names by other children. Then, one day, when he was in college, his father called and asked him to come home immediately because a donor had been found. The boy rushed home and received the operation. It was a great success. The young man graduated from college with honors, and he became a very successful geologist.

One day he received another phone call from his dad, telling him that his mother had suffered a serious heart attack. He rushed home, but it was too late; his mother died before he could get there. Before the funeral, the father took his son to the mortuary. Just the two of them were standing by the casket. Suddenly, the father reached down and brushed back his wife's hair—and the young man saw for the first time that his mother had no right ear!

His father said, "She made me promise never to tell you as long as she lived, but I thought you should know now, that she was the donor who gave you her ear." No one will ever have to explain the meaning of "sacrificial love" to that young man.

Sacrificial love—love that is generous, unconditional, and self-giving. That's what the Christian faith is all about. Jesus showed us that on a cross! When we live in his Spirit, we are building—by his amazing grace—the ark of sacrificial love.

Suggestions for Leading
a Study of

Noah Built His Ark in the Sunshine

John D. Schroeder

This book by James W. Moore is a guide to building an ark of Christian spiritual strengths during the "sunshine" of life, in order to have a better relationship with God and others today and in the years ahead. To assist you in facilitating a discussion group, this study guide was created to help make this experience beneficial for both you and members of your group. Here are some thoughts on how you can help your group:

1. Distribute the book to participants before your first meeting, and request that they come having read the introduction. You may want to limit the size of your group to increase participation.

2. Begin your sessions on time. Your participants will appreciate your promptness. You may wish to begin your first session with introductions and a brief get-acquainted time. Start each session by reading aloud the snapshot summary of the chapter for the day.

3. Select discussion questions and activities in advance. Note that the first question is a general question designed to get discussion going. The last question is designed to summarize the discussion. Feel free to change the order of the listed questions and to create your own questions. Allow a set amount of time for the questions and activities.

4. Remind your participants that all questions are valid as part of the learning process. Encourage their participation in discussion by saying that there are no "wrong" answers and that all input will be appreciated. Invite participants to share their thoughts, personal stories, and ideas as their comfort level allows.

5. Some questions may be more difficult to answer than others. If you ask a question and no one responds, begin the discussion by venturing an answer yourself. Then ask for comments and other answers. Remember that some questions may have multiple answers.

6. Ask the question "Why?" or "Why do you believe that?" to help continue a discussion and give it greater depth.

7. Give everyone a chance to talk. Keep the conversation moving. Occasionally you may want to direct a question to a specific person who has been quiet. "Do you have anything to add?" is a good follow-up question to ask another person. If the topic of conversation gets off track, move ahead by asking the next question in your study guide.

8. Before moving from questions to activities, ask group members if they have any questions that have not been answered. Remember that as a leader, you do not have to know all the answers. Some answers may come from group members. Other answers may even need a bit of research. Your job is to keep the discussion moving and to encourage participation.

9. Review the activity in advance. Feel free to modify it or to create your own activity. Encourage participants to try the "At home" activity.

10. Following the conclusion of the activity, close with a brief prayer, praying either the printed prayer from the study guide or a prayer of your own. If your group desires, pause for individual prayer petitions.

11. Be grateful and supportive. Thank group members for their ideas and participation.

12. You are not expected to be a "perfect" leader. Just do the best you can by focusing on the participants and the lesson. God will help you lead this group.
13. Enjoy your time together!

Suggestions for Participants

1. What you will receive from this study will be in direct proportion to your involvement. Be an active participant!
2. Please make it a point to attend all sessions and to arrive on time so that you can receive the greatest benefit.
3. Read the chapter and review the study-guide questions prior to the meeting. You may want to jot down questions you have from the reading, and also answers to some of the study-guide questions.
4. Be supportive and appreciative of your group leader as well as the other members of your group. You are on a journey together.
5. Your participation is encouraged. Feel free to share your thoughts about the material being discussed.
6. Pray for your group and your leader.

Introduction: Noah Built His Ark in the Sunshine

Snapshot Summary

The introduction illustrates how Noah demonstrated faith, gratitude, and spiritual strength—an example for us to follow.

Reflection / Discussion Questions

1. What insights did you receive from this chapter?
2. In your own words, explain what the title of this book means.
3. What impressed you about the story of Dietrich Bonhoeffer?

4. Have you ever been caught unprepared? How did you handle it?
5. How did Noah exhibit his trust in God?
6. Recall a time when you prepared for something. What are some important elements of preparation?
7. What inner resources are important to have to protect you from the storms of life?
8. What did Bonhoeffer and the apostle Paul have in common? What does the author say are the keys to possessing a strong faith?
9. What did you learn about gratitude from the story of Noah?
10. What key learning from this chapter will you most reflect on in your personal life today / this week?

Activities

As a group: Make a list of things you can do today to prepare for future storms in life.

At home: Focus on maintaining a spirit of praise and thanks to God all week.

Prayer: *Dear God, we thank you that you are with us during all the storms in life. Help us to be spiritually prepared for the future and to trust in you for all our needs. Amen.*

Chapter 1: Building the Ark of Spiritual Strength

Snapshot Summary

This chapter explores the commitments needed to build spiritual strength that will serve you well in times of crisis.

Reflection / Discussion Questions

1. What insights did you receive from this chapter?

2. What lessons did you learn from the parable of the ten bridesmaids (Matthew 25:1-13)?
3. In your own words, explain what it means to have spiritual strength.
4. What kind of a relationship with God do you want when death nears?
5. Reflect on / discuss the benefits of regular Bible reading.
6. How has reading the Bible strengthened your faith?
7. Share a time when you used prayer to get you through a tough period.
8. Explain what it means to have a personal commitment to Christ.
9. At what times do people especially need spiritual strength? Give some examples.
10. What key learning from this chapter will you most reflect on in your personal life today / this week?

Activities

As a group: Make a list of daily activities that build spiritual strength.

At home: Take an inventory, or write a brief essay or journal entry regarding: What is the current status of your spiritual strength?

Prayer: *Dear God, there are things that can't be borrowed, and one of them is spiritual strength. Help us to grow stronger in our faith. Thank you for your love and guidance. Amen.*

Chapter 2: Building the Ark of Compassion

Snapshot Summary

This chapter explores the power of caring and shows how compassion can heal.

Reflection / Discussion Questions

1. What insights did you receive from this chapter?
2. Share an incident where you were too careful.
3. What does having compassion mean to you? Give an example.
4. Why do you think people sometimes lack compassion? List some reasons.
5. Share a time when you were touched by the healing power of caring.
6. How did Jesus heal the woman in Mark 5 socially? Name a contemporary example of social healing.
7. Recall a time when you realized too late that you had lacked compassion.
8. How can caring bring about spiritual healing?
9. Can one truly have compassion without taking action? Why or why not?
10. What key learning from this chapter will you most reflect on in your personal life today / this week?

Activities

As a group: Discuss the costs and benefits of having compassion for others.

At home: Practice compassion and caring in specific ways this week.

Prayer: *Dear God, fill us with compassion and love for others. Help us to heal the wounded through caring, prayer, and acts of kindness. Thank you for showing us compassion and giving us examples to live by. Amen.*

Chapter 3: Building the Ark of Peace

Snapshot Summary

This chapter guides us in how to live in a world at war while working for global peace.

Reflection / Discussion Questions

1. What insights did you receive from this chapter?
2. How have you personally been touched by war?
3. What comes to mind when you view coverage of war protests on television, or read about it in headlines or articles?
4. How are people of the world both different and similar? List differences and similarities.
5. Discuss the four basic approaches to war outlined by the author. Among these, where do you agree and disagree?
6. What role can prayer play in bringing about world peace?
7. In what ways has the world become a global village? Give some examples.
8. Discuss and list some of the causes of war. What do you believe is the major cause?
9. How do you maintain a strong faith in tough times?
10. What key learning from this chapter will you most reflect on in your personal life today / this week?

Activities

As a group: Discuss ways in which people can work for peace in the world.

At home: Meditate on the thought that the way to lasting peace resides in Jesus Christ, the Prince of Peace.

Prayer: *Dear God, we thank you for faith that rises above the troubles of this world. Help bring peace to our world. Show our leaders the path to resolving differences without war. May your love be reflected in our thoughts and deeds. Amen.*

Chapter 4: Building the Ark of Christian Love

Snapshot Summary

This chapter encourages us to love others rather than seeking to control them.

Reflection / Discussion Questions

1. What insights did you receive from this chapter?
2. What's the difference between Christian love and other types of love?
3. Give an example of how you were a recipient of Christian love.
4. How does it feel when you practice Christian love? Describe the feeling.
5. In your own words, explain what "being more than conquerors" means to you. What behavioral traits make Christians more than conquerors?
6. What characteristics are found in good parents?
7. What characteristics are found in someone who is a good mate?
8. In what ways do people try to conquer God?
9. How can Christians be victors even when they are victims?
10. What key learning from this chapter will you most reflect on in your personal life today / this week?

Activities

As a group: List specific ways in which people can be more than conquerors in their life at home, in the church, and/or in the community.

At home: Make specific efforts to practice Christian love this week.

Prayer: *Dear God, we thank you for all of the wonderful people who are a part of our lives. Help us to treat them with respect and caring. May we love others rather than seeking to control them. In Jesus' name. Amen.*

Chapter 5: Building the Ark of Strong Foundations

Snapshot Summary

This chapter explores truth, love, and God as foundations that Christians can always count on.

Reflection / Discussion Questions

1. What insights did you receive from this chapter?
2. Discuss the benefits of having a firm foundation in your life.
3. How can you tell the difference between a weak foundation and a strong foundation?
4. What people do you count on, and why do you count on them?
5. Share a time when you searched for the truth.
6. As a child, what were your firm foundations?
7. Discuss why love is such an important foundation. Whose love can you count upon?
8. How can you make God the foundation of your life?
9. Truth, love, and God are strong foundations. What are others that are important to have in life?
10. What key learning from this chapter will you most reflect on in your personal life today / this week?

Activities

As a group: Discuss ways you can tell what is truth, what is propaganda, and what may be a lie.

At home: Meditate this week on the foundations upon which you are building your life.

Prayer: *Dear God, we thank you for being our strong foundation in the midst of all the turmoil in this world. Help us to seek truth and to practice love as we go about our lives. May we remember that you are always with us. Amen.*

Chapter 6: Building the Ark of Churchmanship

Snapshot Summary

This chapter illustrates the benefits of faithful church attendance and getting involved in the ministry of the church.

Reflection / Discussion Questions

1. What insights did you receive from this chapter?
2. What would your life be like if you did not attend church? Or, what is your life like when you do not attend church?
3. How does—or how would—attending church strengthen you?
4. Can you be a Christian without attending church? Explain.
5. How has church drawn you closer to God?
6. "No institution in the world teaches love and compassion like the church does"; reflect on / discuss this statement.
7. What do you believe are helpful, sensitive ways to respond to persons who feel they have had a "bad experience" in attending church?
8. Give an example of how attending church has increased your compassion for others.
9. With the thought that every church member is called to be in ministry, what are your ministry responsibilities, both inside and outside the church building?
10. What key learning from this chapter will you most reflect on in your personal life today / this week?

Activities

As a group: Discuss why you think Jesus called laypeople and not clergy to be his disciples.

At home: Think about why you attend church. Pray for your church. Consider how you can become a more faithful member.

Prayer: *Dear God, we go to church because that is where we find you and those who love you. Thank you for strengthening our faith. Help us to be more faithful to you and your church. Amen.*

Chapter 7: Building the Ark of Christian Witness

Snapshot Summary

This chapter shows how positive words and actions can be a powerful witness of Christian faith.

Reflection / Discussion Questions

1. What insights did you receive from this chapter?
2. In your own words, explain what it means to be a witness.
3. Why does the world need Christian witnesses?
4. What are the costs and benefits of being a witness?
5. Recall a time when a book you read or a speaker you heard witnessed to you and made an impact.
6. What type of words and what tone of words represent the cause of Christ?
7. What are some words that describe how a Christian should treat others? Make a list.
8. Give an example of Christian service or witness that inspires you.
9. "When we show love, compassion, and kindness to others, that's when they really begin to see our faith"; explain this statement in your own words, and give an example if possible.
10. What key learning from this chapter will you most reflect on in your personal life today / this week?

Activities

As a group: Discuss and list ingredients for being an effective Christian witness.

At home: Think about how you speak to and treat other people. Ask yourself: Am I being a good witness?

Prayer: *Dear God, we thank you for the opportunity to be a witness to your love. You desire that the entire world come to know you. Help us to share the good news with others. May our words and actions be pleasing to you. Amen.*

Chapter 8: Building the Ark of *Kairos* Moments

Snapshot Summary

This chapter explores the power of a *kairos* moment, a time when God touches your soul.

Reflection / Discussion Questions

1. What insights did you receive from this chapter?
2. Explain the difference between *chronos* and *kairos*.
3. What causes a *kairos* moment? How do you experience it?
4. Share a time when you experienced a *kairos* moment.
5. Jesus' life was packed with *kairos* moments. Name some of them. (Feel free to look through the Bible for examples.)
6. How is a person affected by a *kairos* moment of encouragement?
7. Give an example of a *kairos* moment of love. Why do people sometimes miss such moments?
8. Give an example of a *kairos* moment of inspiration.
9. List some words that describe how you feel after a *kairos* moment.
10. What key learning from this chapter will you most reflect on in your personal life today / this week?

Activities

As a group: Locate *kairos* moments in the Old Testament.

At home: Reflect back on the times you experienced a *kairos* moment. Praise God for touching your life.

Prayer: *Dear God, thank you for the special moments in life when we feel so close to you. Help us to treasure these times and to remember them in more difficult days. May we remember that you are always with us, and that you love us more than we can comprehend. Amen.*

Chapter 9: Building the Ark of Confidence

Snapshot Summary

This chapter shows how to avoid being the victim of circumstances, pride, and death.

Reflection / Discussion Questions

1. What insights did you receive from this chapter?
2. Give an example of an incident that helped you gain confidence.
3. In your own words, explain what it means to win an inner victory.
4. What impressed you about the story of Paul in prison?
5. Explain how to avoid becoming a victim of circumstances.
6. Share a time when you were able to rise above circumstances.
7. Explain this statement: "To really live, we have to die to some things first." How does this apply to pride?
8. In what ways do you struggle with pride? How do you deal with it?
9. Explain why Christians do not have to be victims of death.
10. What key learning from this chapter will you most reflect on in your personal life today / this week?

Activities

As a group: Discuss and make a list of some of the great victories in life that have been and are won in the souls of people.

At home: Look for an opportunity to rise above a challenge you are faced with this week.

Prayer: *Dear God, thank you for giving us the confidence to defeat the enemies we face, such as circumstances, pride, and death. Help us to continue to turn challenges into victories and to live with love for others. Amen.*

Chapter 10: Building the Ark of Trust in God

Snapshot Summary

This chapter reminds us of God's presence in the valleys of life.

Reflection / Discussion Questions

1. What insights did you receive from this chapter?
2. Share a troubled time when you felt close to God.
3. What helps you trust in God? What has increased your trust?
4. Is it easier or harder to trust in God as you grow older? Explain.
5. List the valleys in life that most people face. Which valley do you believe is the most difficult for most people?
6. What are some constructive ways to cope with despair?
7. Explain how God's presence turns defeats into victories.
8. How can you reach out and help others during troubled times? List some words and actions that can help.
9. How has God helped comfort you when a friend or family member has died?
10. What key learning from this chapter will you most reflect on in your personal life today / this week?

Activities

As a group: Locate passages in the Bible that are comforting when walking through the valleys of life.

At home: Spend some time this week with someone who may be dealing with tough times.

Prayer: *Dear God, we don't always understand why troubles come our way, but we do understand that you are with us, and we do put our trust in you. Grant us your peace when we are troubled, and help us to minister to others in their times of despair. In Jesus' name. Amen.*

Chapter 11: Building the Ark of Christian Marriage

Snapshot Summary

This chapter looks at the ingredients that go into a loving Christian marriage.

Reflection / Discussion Questions

1. What insights did you receive from this chapter?
2. Reflect on / discuss the four types of communication and their importance.
3. When it comes to communication, what are your strengths and weaknesses?
4. In your own words, describe a healthy Christian marriage.
5. Discuss the importance of continuous courtship.
6. What's wrong with a trial marriage mind-set?
7. Discuss the costs and the benefits of making a marriage commitment.
8. What do you think is the toughest part of marriage? Explain your response.
9. Why are Christ and the church needed to have a great marriage?
10. What key learning from this chapter will you most reflect on in your personal life today / this week?

Activities

As a group: Explore what the Bible says relating to maintaining a healthy marriage.

At home: If you are married, do a self-evaluation of the health of your marriage. If you are single, do a self-evaluation of the health of your relationships with the persons in your life who mean the most to you.

Prayer: *Dear God, we thank you for the gift of marriage. We ask that you protect marriages in these troubled times, and that you help couples realize the power of love. Help us to remember that Christ is the head of every household. Amen.*

Chapter 12: Building the Ark of Purpose

Snapshot Summary

This chapter explores the choices people make that determine a sense of purpose.

Reflection / Discussion Questions

1. What insights did you receive from this chapter?
2. When you were a child, what did you want to do or be when you grew up, and why?
3. Why is a sense of purpose important?
4. What role does your attitude play in determining your choice of purpose?
5. Reflect on / discuss this statement: Life is more than an endurance or survival test. What role does risk play in life?
6. What happens when you build your life around pursuing pleasure?
7. How do money and possessions often act as blinders? Where's the line between pursuing financial security and living a life of overabundance?

8. What happens to people who lack a purpose in life?
9. How did you determine your purpose in life? Has your purpose changed over the years, and if so, how?
10. What key learning from this chapter will you most reflect on in your personal life today / this week?

Activities

As a group: Reflect on / discuss: What is your purpose? Share your plans, hopes, and dreams for the rest of your life.

At home: Meditate on the question, "Friend, why are you here?" (Matthew 26:50 RSV).

Prayer: *Dear God, we thank you for giving us purpose, love, and support as we go about our daily lives. Guide us so that we may be able to separate what is important from those things that are trivial. Help us to see the big picture and not to be blinded by the sights and sounds of our world. Continue to surround us with your love. Amen.*

Chapter 13: Building the Ark of Freedom

Snapshot Summary

This chapter celebrates the freedom God gives us to take action and really live.

Reflection / Discussion Questions

1. What insights did you receive from this chapter?
2. List reasons why people needlessly wait for permission.
3. What impressed you about the story of the woman healed by Jesus?
4. What did you need permission to do as a child? as a teenager?
5. Share a time when you realized you didn't need to wait for permission and used your freedom to take action.

6. Give an example of standing tall for what is right.
7. Why is it important to accept the permission Christ gives us to forgive others?
8. What are some reasons why people wait for permission to start over again? What benefits can "starting over" have compared to simply "starting out"?
9. Give some examples of how God has set you free.
10. What key learning from this chapter will you most reflect on in your personal life today / this week?

Activities

As a group: Reflect on / discuss: God gives us freedom. What responsibilities accompany that freedom? List as many as you can.

At home: Meditate on what you may be waiting for permission to act upon. Know that God has set you free and gives you freedom to act.

Prayer: *Dear God, we thank you for the precious gift of freedom, and for the example Jesus has shown to us of grace, mercy, and forgiveness. Help us to use our freedom wisely and to live as responsible Christians. Amen.*

Chapter 14: Building the Ark of Perseverance

Snapshot Summary

This chapter explores why people break commitments and offers solutions for hanging on and keeping the faith.

Reflection / Discussion Questions

1. What insights did you receive from this chapter?
2. Share a time when you decided to quit something. Was it a good or bad decision?

3. What should people do or remember when they think of giving up? How can practicing perseverance make you stronger?
4. Sometimes it is the right decision to drop out or quit. How do you know whether to quit or to persevere?
5. Should disagreement be handled differently within the church than elsewhere? Explain. What are some of the answers for how to disagree without being disagreeable?
6. Share a time when you felt left out. In what ways can we be sensitive to persons who feel left out?
7. For what reasons can people sometimes feel that God has let them down?
8. How has God helped you persevere?
9. Share a time when you practiced perseverance and were glad you did.
10. What key learning from this chapter will you most reflect on in your personal life today / this week?

Activities

As a group: Reflect on / discuss what the church and church members can do to encourage others to persevere in their faith.

At home: Explore the Bible to find examples of perseverance.

Prayer: *Dear God, we often have trouble with perseverance. Sometimes it is tempting to quit and to take what we think is the easy way out. Give us wisdom and grant us perseverance to do your will and what is right. Thank you for supporting us and being with us as we make our choices in life. Amen.*

Chapter 15: Building the Ark of Sacrificial Love

Snapshot Summary

This chapter encourages us to minister to others and to imitate Christ's gracious ways.

Reflection / Discussion Questions

1. What insights did you receive from this chapter?
2. In your own words, explain what sacrificial love means to you.
3. Give an example of a time when you were the recipient of sacrificial love.
4. List and briefly reflect on / discuss the three characteristics of sacrificial love as outlined by the author.
5. What sometimes prevents people from practicing generosity, from giving of themselves?
6. Why is it often hard for us to love unconditionally? What sorts of conditions do we tend to place upon love?
7. In your own words, what characterizes a relationship of unconditional love? Can you give an example?
8. What motivates Christians to practice sacrificial love?
9. What key learning from this chapter will you most reflect on in your personal life today / this week?
10. What did you learn from reading this book? Share some highlights.

Activities

As a group: List and discuss opportunities for practicing sacrificial love in your church and / or community.

At home: Look for an opportunity to practice sacrificial love this week.

Prayer: *Dear God, thank you for the love and support you show to each one of us. Bless us as we go about our lives, and help us to make the most of opportunities to show your sacrificial love to others. Be with us as we continue to experience your gift of life. In Jesus' name. Amen.*